VYAPAR

AN ENTREPRENEUR'S JOURNEY
FROM IDEA TO SUCCESS

NIKHIL SHANKAR DULHANI

INDIA • SINGAPORE • MALAYSIA

ISBN 979-8-89322-908-0

To my beloved family, friends, and especially my loving daughter Sanskrit.

Contents

Introduction

Welcome to a journey that traverses the thrilling landscape of entrepreneurship. Within the pages of this book, you will embark on an exploration of the dynamic world of business, guided by case studies inspired by the real-life experiences of entrepreneurs who have navigated the tumultuous seas of startups and emerged triumphant.

Vyāpār: An Entrepreneur's Journey from Idea to Success is more than just a book. It is a compendium of lessons learned, challenges overcome, and milestones achieved. It is a testament to the indomitable spirit of entrepreneurship, the relentless pursuit of innovation, and the unyielding resilience in the face of adversity.

This book is not merely a theoretical exploration of business concepts. Instead, it brings to you practical insights gleaned from the trenches of the business world. It offers a unique blend of inspirational narratives and pragmatic advice, packed with real-world examples that highlight the application of business theories in actual scenarios.

Each case study contained in this book is a narrative of an entrepreneur's journey, starting from the conception of an idea, through the arduous process of nurturing that idea into a viable business, to the ultimate realisation of success. These stories will provide you with invaluable insights into the entrepreneurial process, offering you a roadmap to navigate your own entrepreneurial journey.

This book will inspire you, challenge you, and equip you with the knowledge and skills required to transform your entrepreneurial dreams into reality. It presents a holistic view of the business landscape, covering various aspects such as marketing strategies, financial planning, operational efficiency, and leadership skills - all critical elements in the journey from idea to success.

Whether you are a seasoned entrepreneur seeking fresh perspectives, a budding businessperson gearing up for a new venture, or a business enthusiast keen on understanding the intricacies of entrepreneurship, this book is for you.

Prepare yourself for an engaging, enlightening, and empowering journey into the heart of entrepreneurship as you turn the pages of *Vyāpār: An Entrepreneur's Journey from Idea to Success*. Welcome aboard!

Chapter 1

THE BIRTH OF AN IDEA

THE SPARK

In the heart of Mumbai, a young entrepreneur named Ishaan was in the throes of a significant crisis. His startup, a promising venture in the technology sector, was on the brink of collapse. The capital was dwindling, the team was in disarray, and his vision seemed to blur. It was a classic case of a promising idea failing to meet the harsh realities of the business world. In such a dire situation, Ishaan was on the verge of giving up, ready to accept defeat.

However, one day, while he was aimlessly wandering across the city, trying to clear his mind, he found himself standing in front of a small antique shop. Drawn by an inexplicable curiosity, he decided to step inside. The shop was a time capsule filled with relics of the past. As he was browsing through the items, an old brass lamp caught his attention. It was a beautiful piece, with intricate carvings and a sense of history that intrigued him. On an impulse, he decided to buy it.

Back at his office, he placed the lamp on his desk. Looking at the lamp, he was reminded of the fable of Aladdin and his magic lamp. He jokingly rubbed the lamp, half expecting a genie to pop out and grant him three wishes to save his failing business. Of course, there was no genie or magic, but something did happen. As he held the lamp, he experienced a sudden spark of inspiration, a new perspective on his business model that he had never considered before.

Ishaan realised that his business was not failing because of a lack of funds or a faulty product; it was failing because he was trying to fit his unique idea into a conventional business model. His vision was not meant to follow the traditional path; it was meant to create a new one. This revelation was a game-changer for Ishaan. He decided to pivot his business model, aligning it more closely with his original vision.

With renewed vigour, Ishaan started restructuring his startup. He shared his new vision with his team, and they rallied behind him. They began to rework their strategies, focusing on innovation and uniqueness rather than trying to conform to the established norms. Slowly but surely, the startup began showing signs of revival. The team was more motivated, their product started gaining traction, and investors began showing interest.

The journey was still challenging, but Ishaan was no longer afraid of the hurdles. He had found his spark, his guiding light in the form of an antique lamp. The lamp served as a constant reminder that sometimes, the key to success lies in embracing one's uniqueness and not being afraid to chart a new path.

This was the spark that ignited the resurrection of Ishaan's startup. It was not a magic lamp or a genie but a sudden burst of inspiration that came from an unexpected source. It was a testament to the fact that sometimes, all it takes to turn things around is a fresh perspective, a new way of looking at things.

The story of Ishaan and his startup serves as a powerful case study in the business world. It underlines the importance of innovation, adaptability, and the courage to follow one's vision, even when the odds are stacked against you. After all, it is often in the face of adversity that the most brilliant ideas are born and the most successful businesses are built.

NURTURING THE CONCEPT

With the birth of a new business idea, the journey of a thousand miles begins with the first step, and that initial stride is nurturing the concept. This essential phase is where the seed of an idea is watered with intensive research, strategic planning, and critical thinking. It is the stage where the entrepreneur seeks to grow their idea from a mere thought into a viable business proposition.

In the case of Netflix, the idea was conceived when co-founder Reed Hastings was frustrated with a $40 late fee from Blockbuster for a DVD rental. This seemingly insignificant event sparked an idea - what if there were a way to rent movies that didn't involve late fees, due dates, or a run to the video store? An idea was born, but it needed nurturing to grow and evolve into what Netflix is today – a global streaming giant.

Nurturing a concept involves extensive market research to understand the industry, the competition, and the potential customers. It requires understanding the existing pain points in the market and how your business idea can address them. For Netflix, the pain points were clear - late fees, due dates, and the inconvenience of physically going to a rental store.

The next step in nurturing the concept is to develop a unique value proposition. What makes your business idea unique and better than the existing solutions in the market? For Netflix, it was unlimited rentals without due dates or late fees with the convenience of getting DVDs by mail.

However, nurturing a business concept is not a one-time activity; it requires continuous refinement and evolution. With the advent of faster internet speeds and changing consumer preferences, Netflix realised that the future was in online streaming. This was a significant pivot from their original business model, but it was a necessary evolution to stay relevant and competitive.

Part of nurturing a concept also involves building a robust business model. How will the business make money? What are the revenue streams? What are the costs? For Netflix, the revenue model was subscription-based, which guaranteed recurring income and helped in predicting future revenues.

Risk assessment is another crucial aspect of nurturing a business concept. Every business idea comes with its set of risks. Identifying these risks early on and finding ways to mitigate them is essential for the survival and success of the business. For Netflix, one of the significant risks was the dependence on postal services to deliver DVDs. They mitigated this risk by setting up distribution centres across the US to ensure fast delivery.

Lastly, nurturing a concept involves creating a roadmap for execution. This includes planning the resources, timelines, and milestones for turning the business idea into reality. In the case of Netflix, they started with DVD rentals in the US, gradually expanded to streaming, and then produced their content, step by step, following their roadmap.

Nurturing a concept is the first and one of the most crucial steps in the journey of a business. It is the stage where the entrepreneur shapes their idea, validates its potential, and plans its execution. It is where the foundation of a successful business is laid. Netflix's journey from a DVD rental service to a global streaming giant is a testament to the power of nurturing a business concept.

MARKET RESEARCH

In the world of business, it is often said that knowledge is power. This saying rings particularly true in the context of the vital practice of market research. This process, which involves gathering, analysing, and interpreting information about a market, a product or service to be offered for sale in that market, and about the past, present, and potential customers for the product or service, is the lifeblood of any successful business venture.

To fully appreciate the role that market research plays in business, it is instructive to take a closer look at a few case studies.

Consider, for instance, the case of a small, family-run bakery in a mid-sized city. The owners, noticing a decline in sales, decided to conduct market research to identify the root cause of their dwindling profits. They sent out surveys to their customers, conducted focus groups, and studied their sales data meticulously. The results were enlightening. It turned out that a new bakery had opened in town, offering a wider variety of gluten-free and vegan options, which were becoming increasingly popular in their community. Armed with this knowledge, the bakery was able to adapt its product offering and marketing strategy, resulting in a significant increase in sales.

In a different sector, the case of a technology startup offers another compelling illustration of the power of market research. Before launching their new app, the startup's founders conducted extensive market research to identify their target audience, understand their needs and preferences, and study the competitive landscape. This enabled them to tailor their product, pricing, and marketing strategy to their intended market, greatly increasing their chances of success.

The app quickly gained traction, and the startup was eventually acquired by a major technology company.

These examples underscore the importance of market research in identifying and understanding market trends, customer preferences, and competitive threats. However, it is equally important to note that market research is not a one-time activity. Markets are dynamic and constantly evolving, thus necessitating ongoing research to stay abreast of changes and adapt accordingly.

Moreover, market research is not just for large corporations with deep pockets. With the advent of the internet and social media, even small businesses and startups can conduct effective market research without breaking the bank. Online surveys, social media analytics, and website traffic data are just a few of the tools that are now readily available to businesses of all sizes.

In conclusion, market research is an essential practice for any business looking to succeed in today's competitive marketplace. It provides invaluable insights into market trends, customer behaviour, and competitive dynamics, enabling businesses to make informed decisions and strategies. Whether you are a small business owner looking to grow your customer base, a startup founder launching a new product, or a corporate executive seeking to expand into a new market, market research is a powerful tool that can help you achieve your business goals.

VALIDATING THE IDEA

In our journey through the realm of business case studies, we've arrived at a critical juncture where a spark of an idea has been ignited. Now, the question that lies ahead of us is - How do we know if this idea holds the potential to take flight or if it will fizzle out like a damp squib? This is the phase of idea validation, a critical step in the process of business planning.

Imagine yourself standing at the edge of a precipice, holding a paper plane. You've meticulously folded it, and you believe it's ready for flight. But how can you be sure? You could throw it and see if it soars, or it might plummet. Similarly, in business, you can't just launch an idea without testing its viability. You need to validate your idea to ensure it's not just a paper plane but a fully-fledged jet ready for take off.

Let's delve deeper into the case of 'R Rides,' a bike-sharing company. The founders, Aryan and Aastha, were confident that their idea of providing eco-friendly, health-conscious transportation in their city was a winner. But they knew that to transform their idea into a successful venture, they needed more than just confidence. They needed validation.

Aryan and Aastha started by conducting market research. They aimed to understand their potential customers, their needs, preferences, and pain points. They distributed surveys, conducted interviews, and initiated focus group discussions. Their findings revealed a growing trend towards eco-friendly transportation and health consciousness, particularly among millennials. This gave them the first indication that their idea might just work.

Next, they analysed their competition. They wanted to understand how other bike-sharing services operated, what they offered, and how they could differentiate R Rides. They found that while there were other bike-sharing services, none focused on the eco-friendly and health-conscious angle. This gap in the market gave them a unique selling proposition and further validated their idea.

However, validation isn't just about the external environment. Aryan and Aastha needed to ensure that their idea was feasible internally as well. They needed to consider their resources, capabilities, and constraints. They evaluated their financial ability to start the business, their technical expertise to maintain the bikes, and their managerial skills to operate the business. After a thorough analysis, they concluded that they had the necessary resources and skills to make R Rides a reality.

Finally, they decided to test their idea in the real world. They launched a small pilot project in a part of their city. The response was overwhelming. People loved the concept, and R Rides became an instant hit. This successful pilot run was the final validation they needed.

So, did Aryan and Aastha's paper plane fly? It did more than just fly. It soared high, all because they took the time to validate their idea.

This chapter on idea validation has demonstrated that while an idea may seem brilliant in your head, it's essential to validate it in the real world. Market research, competitive analysis, internal feasibility, and real-world testing are all crucial components of this process. So, before you launch your idea, make sure you've validated it. Don't just throw your paper plane off a cliff and hope it flies. Test it, validate it, and then watch it soar.

Chapter 2

PLANNING THE VENTURE

BUSINESS MODEL

Once upon a time, in Delhi, there was a thriving business that stood out from the rest - 'Innovate Inc.' This company was known far and wide for its unique approach to business, a model that was as effective as it was innovative. The tale of Innovate Inc.'s business model speaks of vision, determination, and strategic planning.

The company's business model was not built overnight. It was the brainchild of the company's founder, a visionary named Tushar. Tushar understood that a successful business model is like a well-oiled machine, with every part working in harmony to produce a desirable result. He knew that a business model was not just about selling a product or service; it was about creating value for customers, employees, and stakeholders alike.

Innovate Inc.'s business model was built upon three key pillars: innovation, customer-centricity, and sustainability.

Innovation was at the very heart of the company. Tushar believed that in the rapidly evolving world of business, innovation was not just an advantage; it was a necessity. This belief was reflected in the company's relentless pursuit of new ideas, technologies, and strategies. Innovate Inc. was never content with the status quo. It was always looking for ways to improve, to evolve, to innovate.

The second pillar, customer-centricity, was equally important. Tushar understood that a business model that did not put the customer at its centre was doomed to fail. He knew that customers were not just a source of revenue; they were the lifeblood of the business. Thus, every aspect of Innovate Inc.'s business model was designed with the customer in mind. From product development to after-sales service, the customer was always the priority.

The third and final pillar of Innovate Inc.'s business model was sustainability. Tushar believed that a successful business model was not just about making profits in the short-term; it was about ensuring the long-term success and viability of the business. This belief was reflected in the company's commitment to sustainable practices, from its use of renewable resources to its efforts to reduce its carbon footprint.

Innovate Inc.'s business model was a testament to the power of strategic planning and visionary leadership. It was a model that was not only profitable but also sustainable, customer-centric, and innovative. It was a model that other businesses aspired to emulate.

The tale of Innovate Inc.'s business model is a tale of success, a tale of a business that understood the importance of a well-designed business model. It is a tale that serves as a reminder that a business model is not just about making money; it's about creating value for all stakeholders.

In the world of business, a well-crafted business model is like a blueprint for success. It is the foundation upon which a successful business is built. The tale of Innovate Inc.'s business model is a testament to this truth. It is a tale that inspires and educates, a tale that serves as a guide for aspiring entrepreneurs and business leaders. It is a tale that underscores the importance of a well-designed business model in the world of business.

In the end, the story of Innovate Inc. is the story of a business model that worked. It is a story that provides valuable lessons for anyone interested in the world of business. And it is a story that reminds us that in the world of business, a well-crafted business model is not just a tool for success; it is a prerequisite.

BUDGETING

In the bustling heart of Raipur, a young startup, 'TechGen', was beginning to make waves. It was a dynamic company with an innovative product that was rapidly gaining traction. However, the young founders, Deenal and Bani, were facing a significant challenge: managing their finances.

They were exceptional engineers, but when it came to budgeting, they were at a loss. The financial jargon was alien to them, and they found it hard to predict the cash flow, let alone allocate resources efficiently. Realising they needed help, they hired a seasoned finance manager, Nikhil, to guide them through the labyrinth of budgeting.

Nikhil joined TechGen with a wealth of experience in managing finances for startups. He was a firm believer that budgeting was not just about crunching numbers but a strategic tool to guide the company's future. He swiftly set about laying the foundation of a robust budgeting system.

He began by explaining to Deenal and Bani that a budget was essentially a financial plan. It was a roadmap that outlined the company's goals and how they planned to achieve them.

It also served as a tool to monitor the company's performance and ensure they were on the right track.

Nikhil stressed the importance of realistic budgeting. He cautioned against over-optimistic projections that could lead to overspending and financial distress. He emphasised that a budget should be flexible and capable of adapting to unforeseen changes. He also highlighted that it was crucial to involve all departments in the budgeting process to ensure buy-in and commitment.

Nikhil introduced the concept of zero-based budgeting, where every expenditure had to be justified for each new period. This approach, he explained, encouraged efficiency and accountability, as it prevented wasteful spending and complacency.

However, Nikhil also warned of its drawbacks. It was a time-consuming process and could lead to short-term thinking, as departments might be reluctant to spend on long-term projects for fear of not getting approval in the next budget.

Next, Nikhil introduced the concept of incremental budgeting, where the previous period's budget was used as a base, and adjustments were made based on the expected changes for the upcoming period. This approach was less time-consuming and provided stability and predictability. However, it could also lead to inefficiencies, as it did not encourage departments to scrutinise their spending.

Nikhil emphasised that there was no one-size-fits-all approach. The choice of budgeting method depended on the company's context, culture, and strategic objectives.

With Nikhil's guidance, Deenal and Bani began to see budgeting in a new light. It was no longer a daunting task but a strategic tool that could help them steer their startup towards success. They realised that budgeting was not just about controlling costs but about making informed decisions that balanced the company's short-term needs with its long-term goals.

As TechGen continued to grow, the importance of budgeting became increasingly apparent. It helped the company navigate the volatile startup landscape, manage its resources efficiently, and stay on track towards its strategic objectives. Deenal and Bani were grateful for Nikhil's guidance, and they realised that budgeting was indeed an integral part of running a successful business.

In the realm of business, budgeting is often seen as a mundane, administrative task. However, as the case of TechGen illustrates, it is a powerful tool that can guide a company's strategic decisions, ensure efficient use of resources, and pave the way for sustained success.

RISK ASSESSMENT

In the labyrinth of business decisions, every turn, every choice, and every action carries a potential risk. The third chapter of our journey through business case studies delves into the realm of risk assessment, a critical process that serves as a guide through this maze.

Imagine a captain steering his ship through a stormy sea. The captain does not merely rely on his gut instincts but employs sophisticated tools and techniques to measure the severity of the storm, the strength of the ship, and the potential paths to safety. Similarly, in the business world, risk assessment is that essential compass, a systematic approach to identifying potential hazards, evaluating their impact, and determining the best course of action to mitigate them.

Take, for instance, the case of a well-known tech giant. At the height of its success, it decided to venture into a new market segment. The product was innovative, the team was passionate, and the projections were optimistic. However, they failed to thoroughly assess the risks associated with this new venture. The result was a product that was ahead of its time, a market that was not ready, and a venture that led to significant financial loss.

In contrast, consider the case of a global beverage company that was planning to introduce a new product line. They conducted a comprehensive risk assessment, examining every possible scenario. They looked at market trends, consumer preferences, and potential supply chain issues. They even considered unforeseen circumstances like natural disasters and political unrest. This thorough risk assessment allowed them to identify potential pitfalls and develop contingency plans. When they finally launched their product, they were prepared for all eventualities, leading to a successful and profitable venture.

Risk assessment is not a one-size-fits-all solution. Each business, each decision, and each situation is unique. It requires a deep understanding of the business, its environment, and its stakeholders. It demands a clear and objective analysis of the potential risks and their implications. It necessitates a commitment to regular re-evaluation and adjustment.

But why is risk assessment so important? Because it helps businesses make informed decisions. It allows them to weigh the potential benefits against the potential risks. It equips them with the knowledge and the tools to navigate through the stormy seas of business uncertainties. It empowers them to seize opportunities without being blindsided by potential threats.

However, risk assessment is not just about avoiding pitfalls. It is also about identifying opportunities. It is about turning challenges into stepping stones and uncertainties into catalysts for innovation and growth. It is about creating a resilient and agile business that can not only survive but thrive in a volatile and unpredictable business landscape.

As we journey through the world of business case studies, let us remember that risk assessment is not a destination but a journey. It is a continuous and evolving process that requires vigilance, diligence, and adaptability. It is a compass that guides us through the labyrinth of business decisions, helping us to navigate with confidence and make decisions with conviction. It is, indeed, a critical tool in the toolkit of every successful business.

STRATEGIC PLANNING

As we delve deeper into the intricacies of business case studies, we find ourselves standing at the threshold of an important concept - Strategic Planning. This is the compass that guides businesses; it is the beacon that illuminates the path to success. Strategic planning is the blueprint that every business, regardless of size or industry, must have to navigate through the dynamic and often tumultuous business environment.

Imagine setting sail on a voyage without a map or a compass. The same perilous journey is embarked upon by businesses that operate without strategic planning. It is the process that sets the direction and scope of an enterprise over the long-term, matching its resources to its changing environment and, in particular, its markets, customers, and clients so as to meet stakeholder expectations.

Let us explore the realm of strategic planning with a case study of a renowned company - Apple Inc. The tech giant, known for its innovative products and trend-setting strategies, provides a compelling illustration of strategic planning.

In the late 1990s, Apple was on the brink of bankruptcy. However, the re-appointment of Steve Jobs as the CEO marked a turning point. Jobs, a visionary and a master strategist embarked on a strategic planning journey that would not only rescue Apple but catapult it to the zenith of success. His strategy was simple yet powerful - "Think Different". This became the cornerstone of Apple's strategic planning, leading to the development of groundbreaking products like the iPod, iPhone, and iPad.

Apple's strategic planning focused on creating innovative, high-quality products and services that met customer needs in ways that competitors could not. The company invested heavily in research and development, constantly seeking to push the boundaries of technology and design. It also concentrated on building a strong brand and creating a unique retail experience for customers.

At the heart of Apple's strategic planning was a deep understanding of its customers. It knew that customers did not just want products; they wanted solutions and experiences. This customer-centric approach allowed Apple to anticipate and meet customer needs, often before customers themselves were aware of these needs. Thus, Apple's strategic planning was not merely about surviving in the market but about shaping the market.

However, strategic planning is not a one-time activity. It is a continuous, iterative process that requires constant monitoring and adjustment. Apple's strategic planning evolved over time, adapting to changes in the business environment, technology, and customer preferences. The company's ability to anticipate and adapt to change has been a key factor in its enduring success.

In conclusion, strategic planning is a critical element in the success of a business. It provides direction, facilitates decision-making, and enables businesses to adapt to change. It is not a guarantee of success, but without it, failure is almost certain.

The case of Apple demonstrates the power of strategic planning. It shows us that strategic planning is not just about making plans but about thinking differently, understanding customers, and creating value. It is about having a vision and the courage to pursue that vision, even in the face of adversity. It is about not just surviving but thriving in the competitive business landscape. It is, in essence, the art of business.

Chapter 3
EXECUTING THE PLAN

BUILDING THE TEAM

In the early stages of a business journey, the vision of a single individual is often the driving force that sets the gears in motion. However, as the venture grows, it becomes abundantly clear that a solitary figure cannot sustain the escalating demands of a burgeoning company. This is where the significance of team-building comes into play, a crucial element that is often the difference between success and failure in the business world.

In the case of Tech Innovators Inc., a Silicon Valley-based startup, the founder, Vishal, experienced this firsthand. Vishal was a brilliant software engineer with a revolutionary idea, but his expertise lay in technical matters, not in handling the diverse aspects of running a business. As the company began to gain traction, Vishal found himself overwhelmed, juggling between coding, marketing, finance, and human resources. He soon realised that he needed a team, not just any team, but one that complemented his skills and shared his vision.

The first step Vishal took was identifying the areas where he needed assistance. He was an excellent coder but lacked knowledge in marketing, finance, and human resources. He decided to build a team that could fill these gaps. Vishal wanted individuals who were not just experts in their fields but were also passionate about the company's vision and had an entrepreneurial spirit.

Vishal's first hire was Sakshi, a marketing whiz with experience working with tech startups. Sakshi didn't just bring in marketing expertise; she also brought a fresh perspective on how to position their product in the market. Next, he brought in Dhruv, a seasoned finance professional. Dhruv's role was not just to manage the company's finances but also to steer it towards financial sustainability. Lastly, he hired Salmin, an HR expert, to manage the growing team and ensure a healthy work culture.

Building this team wasn't straightforward. Vishal faced challenges in attracting the right talent due to limited resources and brand recognition. However, he leveraged his vision for the company and the opportunity for the team members to play a significant role in shaping the company's direction as key selling points.

Once the team was in place, the next step was to ensure that they functioned as a cohesive unit. Vishal fostered an open and collaborative culture where ideas were freely exchanged, and everyone's contribution was valued. Regular team meetings were held, not just to discuss business matters but also to build relationships among team members. Vishal also emphasised the importance of understanding and respecting each other's roles, which reduced friction and increased efficiency.

The results were impressive. With a dedicated team, Tech Innovators Inc. could effectively manage its operations and focus on its core competency: innovation. The company's growth accelerated, and it successfully secured funding from prominent venture capitalists.

Vishal's experience underscores the importance of building a balanced team in business. A good team is not just a group of individuals working together. It is a synergistic combination of diverse skills, shared vision, and mutual respect. In the business world, a well-built team can be the engine that propels a company to new heights.

PRODUCT DEVELOPMENT

As the sun began to peek over the horizon, painting the sky with hues of orange and pink, the team at Spark Innovations were already hard at work. The office was buzzing with energy, the air thick with creativity and ambition. This was more than just a place of work; it was a breeding ground for revolutionary ideas that had the potential to change the world.

The team was working on their latest project, a product that aimed to disrupt the market. The stakes were high, and the pressure was on. But the team was not daunted. They knew they had the skills and the passion to bring their vision to life.

Product development was at the heart of Spark Innovations. It was the driving force behind their success. It was a process that started with an idea, a spark of inspiration that was nurtured and developed until it transformed into a tangible product. It was a journey that was as challenging as it was rewarding.

The process of product development was not a linear one. It was a series of steps that were interconnected and often overlapped. It began with the identification of a market need. This was followed by the generation of a product concept to meet that need. Next came the design and development of the product, followed by testing and validation. Finally, the product was launched in the market.

While the process may seem straightforward on paper, it was far from it in reality. Each step was fraught with challenges and uncertainties. The team had to constantly adapt and innovate to overcome these obstacles. Yet, they were undeterred. They knew that every challenge was an opportunity in disguise.

The team at Spark Innovations was diverse, each member bringing a unique set of skills and perspectives to the table. They worked in synergy, their ideas and expertise complementing each other. This diversity was their strength. It allowed them to approach problems from different angles and come up with innovative solutions.

The development of a product was more than just a technical process. It required a deep understanding of the market and the customer. It required the ability to anticipate future trends and adapt to changing needs. It required the courage to take risks and the resilience to bounce back from failures.

As the team worked tirelessly on their project, they knew they were not just creating a product. They were creating a solution, a tool that had the potential to improve lives and make a difference. They were not just developing a product; they were shaping the future.

The journey of product development was a long and arduous one. But the team at Spark Innovations was undeterred. They knew that the journey was as important as the destination. They knew that the challenges they faced were stepping stones to success. They knew that their passion and determination would lead them to create a product that was not just innovative but also impactful.

As the sun set, painting the sky with hues of purple and red, the team at Spark Innovations was still hard at work. Their day was far from over. But they were not weary. They were energised, fuelled by their passion and their vision. They knew they were on the brink of something great. Their product was not just a dream anymore; it was becoming a reality. And they were ready to make their mark on the world.

OPERATIONS MANAGEMENT

As the narrative continues to unfold, we delve deeper into the heart of any successful business - its operations. In the bustling backstage of a thriving company, the spotlight shines on the unsung heroes, the operations managers. Their role is often overlooked, yet it is they who orchestrate the symphony of processes that bring a business to life.

Imagine a busy factory where the hum of machinery is a constant background noise. This is where raw materials are transformed into a product under the watchful eye of the operations manager. They are the director of this industrial ballet, coordinating the dance of production lines, manpower, and machinery. They ensure the rhythm is maintained and the performance is flawless. The job requires a keen eye for detail, a strategic mind, and a robust understanding of the business.

The operations manager's role is not confined to the factory floor. They are also responsible for managing supply chains, ensuring the timely delivery of raw materials, and the distribution of finished products. In our globalised world, this is no mean feat. It involves coordinating with suppliers and distributors across different time zones, navigating through complex customs regulations, and mitigating risks posed by geopolitical uncertainties.

The operations manager is also the custodian of quality. They implement and monitor quality control measures, ensuring that the products meet the high standards set by the company. They are the last line of defence against faulty products reaching the customers, protecting the reputation of the business.

In the world of services, the operations manager plays an equally crucial role. They manage the delivery of services, ensuring that they are provided efficiently and effectively. They coordinate teams of professionals, juggling schedules to meet client needs. They also manage the infrastructure that supports service delivery, from IT systems to physical facilities.

In this digital age, operations management also involves managing information systems. These systems are the nervous system of a business, carrying vital information from one part of the organisation to another. The operations manager ensures that these systems are running smoothly, safeguarding the flow of information.

However, the role of an operations manager is not just about managing processes. It is also about managing people. They lead teams of workers, fostering a culture of productivity and teamwork. They also liaise with other departments, breaking down silos and promoting cross-functional collaboration.

The operations manager is also a key player in strategic planning. They provide valuable input into decision-making, drawing on their intimate knowledge of the business's operational capabilities. They help shape the future direction of the company, aligning operational strategies with business objectives.

In short, operations management is the engine that drives a business. It is about turning ideas into reality, plans into action, and resources into results. It is about making things happen.

In the chapters that follow, we will delve deeper into the world of operations management. We will explore case studies that highlight the challenges and opportunities faced by operations managers in different industries. We will learn from their successes and failures, gaining insights that can be applied to our own businesses.

So, let's embark on this journey into the fascinating world of operations management. Let's discover the magic that happens behind the scenes, where the real business happens.

LAUNCHING THE VENTURE

As we delve deeper into our journey through business case studies, we find ourselves at a critical juncture that can make or break any entrepreneurial endeavour - the launching of the venture. It's akin to setting sail on an uncharted sea, a moment filled with a mix of exhilaration, anticipation, and uncertainty.

Our first case study in this chapter is that of a young entrepreneur named Simran. She had a groundbreaking idea for a sustainable fashion brand. With a solid business plan in hand, she was ready to bring her vision to life. However, the launch of her venture was far from smooth. Simran had underestimated the logistical challenges associated with sourcing sustainable materials, and the initial customer response was lukewarm. It was a stark reminder that even the most foolproof business plans can falter if not executed properly.

Simran's story underscores the importance of meticulous planning and preparation during the venture's launch phase. It's not just about having a brilliant idea or a comprehensive business plan. It's also about understanding the market, anticipating potential roadblocks, and having contingency plans in place.

Our next case brings us to an entirely different industry - technology. We delve into the chronicles of a tech startup named Zen, which shot to fame with its innovative cloud storage solutions. Zen's launch was a textbook example of how to effectively leverage media and public relations to create a buzz in the market.

However, the real game-changer for Zen was its strategic partnerships. By aligning with established tech giants, Zen was able to tap into their customer base and gain credibility. This case study illustrates the power of strategic alliances and the role they can play in a successful venture launch.

But what happens when things don't go as planned during the launch? Our third case study offers some insights. We look at the story of a gourmet food delivery service that started with a bang but soon fizzled out. Hindered by operational inefficiencies and growing competition, the company struggled to keep up with customer expectations.

Despite the initial setback, the company's leadership did not lose hope. They revisited their business model, made necessary changes, and relaunched the service. The second launch, although more subdued, proved more successful in the long run. This case serves as a testament to the fact that a rocky launch does not necessarily spell doom for a venture. With the right mindset and strategic adjustments, businesses can bounce back stronger.

Finally, we explore the story of an online tutoring platform. This venture's launch was unique in that it was entirely virtual, a necessity brought on by the global pandemic. The case study offers valuable insights into launching a venture in a virtual environment, a reality that many entrepreneurs are grappling with in today's digital age.

Each of these stories offers unique insights and learnings on launching a venture. They highlight the importance of preparation, strategic alliances, adaptability, and resilience.

But above all, they remind us that launching a venture is just the beginning of the entrepreneurial journey. It's a crucial step, no doubt, but it's what happens after the launch - the ability to sustain and grow the venture - that ultimately determines its success.

Chapter 4
OVERCOMING CHALLENGES

FINANCIAL HURDLES

As the sun began to set, casting long shadows over the city, Assim, the CEO of a burgeoning tech startup, sat alone in his office. The glow of the city lights outside was a stark contrast to the dimly lit room where Assim was wrestling with his thoughts. The company he had nurtured from its infancy was now teetering on the brink of a precipice. The financial hurdles they were facing seemed insurmountable.

His company, Techtonic, had hit a rough patch. Their innovative product, designed to revolutionise the way businesses operate, was a hit among early adopters. It was hailed as a game-changer, a marvel of modern technology. Investors initially flocked to Techtonic, impressed by its potential for growth and profitability. However, the initial euphoria had faded, replaced by a sobering reality. The cost of production was soaring, and the expected revenue was nowhere in sight.

Assim remembered the early days when he had first pitched his idea to investors. He had been so confident, so sure of the product's success. He had promised them huge returns on their investments and assured them of the product's market demand. However, the market hadn't responded as enthusiastically as he had hoped. The sales were sluggish, and the product, despite its revolutionary features, was struggling to find a foothold in the highly competitive market.

Assim reflected on the financial hurdles his company was facing. They were running out of cash fast. The investors were getting restless, demanding to see results. The production costs were spiralling out of control due to unexpected technical glitches and the high cost of raw materials. The marketing budget was also draining their resources, with the company spending heavily on advertising and promotional activities to boost sales.

The situation was further exacerbated by a sudden economic downturn. The market was shrinking, and businesses were cutting down on their spending. As a result, the demand for Techtonic's product was dwindling. Assim was faced with a challenging task: how to navigate these financial hurdles and steer his company towards profitability.

To add to their woes, Techtonic was also facing stiff competition from other tech startups. These competitors were offering similar products at lower prices, further eating into Techtonic's market share. Assim knew that they couldn't afford to lower their prices without compromising on the quality of their product. It was a classic Catch-22 situation.

Assim's mind raced as he tried to come up with a solution. He knew that they needed to cut down on their costs and find a way to boost sales. He considered seeking additional funding but knew that it would be a tough sell given the company's current financial situation. He also contemplated laying off some of his staff to reduce costs, but the thought of letting go of his hardworking team was heartbreaking.

As Assim grappled with these financial hurdles, he realised the importance of having a solid business plan.

He acknowledged that he had been overly optimistic in his projections and hadn't prepared for such setbacks. He understood that running a business was not just about having a great product; it was also about managing finances effectively, anticipating market trends, and being prepared for any eventuality.

As the night deepened, Assim's resolve strengthened. He knew that the road ahead was tough, but he was not ready to give up. He decided to face these financial hurdles head-on, learn from his mistakes, and steer his company towards success. This was just the first of many business case studies he would encounter in his entrepreneurial journey.

MARKET COMPETITION

In the dynamic world of business, one of the most compelling narratives unfolds within the arena of market competition. Competition is the lifeblood of a market economy, the driving force that fuels innovation, improves quality and lowers prices. It can be a grand drama, a high-stakes game where the players vie for dominance and where the prize is not just profit but survival.

Imagine a bustling marketplace where traders hawk their wares, customers haggle over prices, and the air is filled with the din of commerce. Each trader is a business, each customer is a market, and each transaction is a competition. The traders who offer the best products at the most competitive prices win the customers' patronage, while those who fail to do so risk being pushed out of the market.

Such is the nature of market competition. It's a relentless race where the finish line keeps moving and where the only constant is change. Businesses must continually adapt and innovate or risk being overtaken by their competitors. It's a Darwinian struggle where only the fittest survive.

Let us delve into some real-world case studies that illustrate this narrative.

Consider the story of Kodak, once a titan in the photography industry. For decades, Kodak dominated the market with its film cameras. But when digital cameras arrived, Kodak was slow to adapt. It clung to its film cameras even as its competitors embraced the new technology. As a result, Kodak lost its market dominance and eventually filed for bankruptcy. The Kodak story is a cautionary tale of what can happen when a business fails to adapt to market competition.

On the other end of the spectrum is the story of Netflix, a company that has thrived in the face of fierce market competition. Netflix started as a DVD rental service, but when the market shifted towards online streaming, Netflix was quick to adapt. It invested heavily in its streaming platform and original content, and today, it's one of the leading players in the online streaming market. The Netflix story is an inspiring example of how a business can leverage market competition to drive innovation and growth.

Market competition is not just about battling rivals, though. It's also about understanding the needs and wants of the customers. A business that can anticipate and meet the changing demands of its customers can gain a competitive edge.

Take the case of Amazon, for instance. Amazon has consistently stayed ahead of its competitors by focusing on customer satisfaction. It offers a wide range of products, fast delivery, and excellent customer service. As a result, Amazon has managed to retain a large and loyal customer base despite intense market competition.

In the grand narrative of market competition, businesses rise and fall, markets evolve, and customers' needs change. It's a fascinating saga, a tale of triumphs and failures, of innovation and obsolescence, of strategic moves and tactical blunders. It's a story that offers valuable lessons for businesses and one that underscores the importance of adaptability, innovation, and customer focus in the face of market competition.

OPERATIONAL DIFFICULTIES

As the morning sun seeped through the blinds of the corner office, CEO Amit sat with his head in his hands, a stack of quarterly reports forming a fortress around him. The numbers were clear: operational inefficiencies were threatening to sink the company he had built from the ground up.

The company's production line had been a well-oiled machine, delivering quality products on time, every time. But in recent quarters, the gears had started to grind. Inventory was piling up, orders were being delayed, and a once harmonious workflow had devolved into a chaotic scramble.

Amit knew that the root of these operational difficulties lay in the company's rapid expansion. With the increase in demand, they had hastily scaled up their operations. The once efficient assembly line was now a sprawling network of disjointed units, each marching to its own beat. The company's IT infrastructure, too, was stretched thin, struggling to keep up with the demands of a much larger operation.

The toll of these operational difficulties was evident in the company's bottom line. Profits were dwindling, customer complaints were on the rise, and employee morale was at an all-time low. Amit knew that to weather this storm, he needed to identify the operational bottlenecks and implement effective solutions.

He started with the production line. A thorough analysis revealed that the primary bottleneck was at the assembly stage, where a lack of coordination and communication between different units led to delays and errors. To tackle this, Amit decided to invest in a state-of-the-art production management system. This system would streamline the workflow, ensuring that all units worked in harmony and that any potential issues were flagged in real-time.

Next, he turned his attention to the company's IT infrastructure. The current system was outdated and unable to support the company's expanded operations. Recognising the critical role of IT in modern-day business operations, Amit decided to overhaul the company's IT infrastructure. He brought in a team of experts to design and implement a robust, scalable system that would not only meet the company's current needs but also support future growth.

Amit's measures didn't stop at technological upgrades. He knew that the company's most valuable resource was its workforce. To boost morale and productivity, he introduced a series of initiatives aimed at improving employee satisfaction. These included flexible working hours, training programmes, and a revamped reward system.

The journey to overcoming operational difficulties was not easy, and the results did not come overnight. But Amit's decisive actions and unwavering commitment to operational efficiency gradually turned the tide. The production line was humming again, customer complaints were down, and the company was back on track to profitability.

As Amit looked out of his office window at the bustling factory floor, he knew that the company's operational difficulties had been a blessing in disguise. They had forced him to take a hard look at his operations and make necessary improvements. The company was now stronger, more resilient, and better equipped to handle whatever challenges lay ahead.

In the world of business, operational difficulties are an inevitable part of the journey. However, as Amit's story shows, with the right approach, these challenges can be transformed into opportunities for growth and improvement.

CRISIS MANAGEMENT

It was a typical Monday morning in the bustling city of Bengaluru. The CEO of a renowned multinational company, Mr. Rishi, sipped his coffee while going through the morning's headlines. Suddenly, his phone buzzed with a flurry of messages and emails. He glanced at the screen, and his heart skipped a beat. A leading news outlet had just published a story alleging unethical practices within his company. His company was in the midst of a crisis.

He immediately summoned his core team - the CFO, the head of HR, the head of PR, and the company's legal counsel. As he explained the situation, the room fell silent. The company, they all knew, was on the brink of a major crisis. The allegations, true or not, could tarnish the company's reputation. Their shares could plummet, investors could back out, and they could lose their hard-earned market position.

As the leader, Mr Rishi knew he had to steer his team out of this crisis. He remembered a case study he had read in business school about a company that had successfully managed a similar situation. He decided to follow a similar path. He understood that crisis management wasn't just about damage control; it was about turning the crisis into an opportunity for growth.

He started by setting up a crisis management team with representatives from each department. Their first task was to gather all the facts and understand the severity of the situation. They needed to know exactly what they were dealing with before they could formulate a response.

Meanwhile, he instructed the PR team to issue a statement acknowledging the allegations and promising a thorough investigation. He knew that transparency and honesty were crucial in such situations. He also reached out to the leading news outlet and offered an exclusive interview. He wanted to take control of the narrative before it spun out of control.

Over the next few weeks, the crisis management team worked tirelessly. They conducted an internal audit and found some minor discrepancies but nothing as severe as the allegations. They also identified several areas for improvement in their business practices. They took this as an opportunity to strengthen their internal processes and ensure such a situation would never arise again.

Mr. Rishi, in his interview, admitted to the discrepancies and emphasised the corrective measures they were taking. He assured stakeholders that they were committed to ethical business practices and that the current crisis was a wake-up call for them.

The company's handling of the crisis was praised by industry experts. Their shares, which had initially taken a hit, started to recover. Their transparent and proactive approach helped them regain their stakeholders' trust.

The crisis, while initially seeming disastrous, had become an opportunity for growth. The company emerged stronger, with improved business practices and a renewed commitment to ethics.

Crisis management, as this case study illustrates, is not just about navigating through a crisis. It's about using the crisis as a catalyst for change and improvement. It's about turning a threat into an opportunity.

Chapter 5

EXPANDING THE BUSINESS

MARKET DIVERSIFICATION

As our journey into the business world unfolds, we encounter a robust and versatile strategy known as market diversification. It's a strategy that has become a cornerstone for many successful businesses, and it's one that we'll explore in depth in this chapter.

Imagine, if you will, a thriving business that has gained substantial market share in its industry. This business, let's call it Company A, has been selling a single product, but its leadership team is considering expanding the product line. They realise that the market is dynamic and unpredictable. Depending solely on one product can make them vulnerable to changes in market trends, economic fluctuations, and aggressive competition. They decide to diversify their market.

In the simplest terms, market diversification is akin to the old adage, "Don't put all your eggs in one basket." It's a risk management strategy that involves expanding product offerings or penetrating into new markets to broaden the customer base and increase revenue streams.

Let's delve deeper into Company A's decision to diversify. The team begins by conducting comprehensive market research. They identify gaps in the market and seek to understand potential customers' needs. They also analyse their competitors' strategies and the overall market environment.

Armed with this knowledge, Company A decides to introduce a new product. They don't venture too far from their original offering, but they ensure that the new product appeals to a different customer segment. The goal here is to spread the risk. If one product faces a downturn, the other can potentially offset the loss.

Market diversification isn't without its challenges. It requires significant investment, both in terms of time and money. It also demands a robust understanding of the new markets or products. Moreover, the company risks diluting its brand if the new product or market doesn't align with its existing identity.

Company A, however, is undeterred. They recognise the potential rewards and proceed with caution. They invest in marketing campaigns to raise awareness about their new product. They train their sales team to effectively sell to the new market segment. They also ensure that their supply chain and operations can handle the expanded product line.

As time progresses, Company A starts to see positive results. Their customer base grows, and so do their revenues. The new product has not only provided an additional revenue stream but also helped buffer the company against market volatility.

Market diversification has proven to be a successful strategy for Company A, but it's important to note that it may not work for all businesses. It requires careful planning, diligent execution, and continuous monitoring. It's not just about adding more products or entering new markets; it's about making strategic choices that align with the company's overall goals and capabilities.

In the end, market diversification is a business strategy that can lead to growth and stability. It allows a company to spread its risk across different products and markets, making it less vulnerable to market fluctuations and competitive pressures. It's a strategy that has enabled many businesses to thrive in an ever-changing business landscape.

As we close this chapter, we hope that you've gained a deeper understanding of market diversification and its role in business success. In the next chapter, we'll explore another key business strategy, providing you with more tools to navigate the complex world of business.

PRODUCT LINE EXTENSION

Once upon a time, in the bustling city of Kolhapur, a small bakery named "Sweet Delights." This bakery was known far and wide for its heavenly melt-in-the-mouth cookies. The owner, Shreya, was a diligent woman who believed in the power of innovation and was always on the lookout for ways to expand her business.

One day, at the break of dawn, as the aroma of freshly baked cookies wafted through the air, Shreya had an epiphany. She realised that while her cookies were the talk of the town, there were other sweet treats she could introduce to attract a wider customer base. This was the beginning of her journey into the realm of product line extension.

Shreya decided to extend her product line from cookies to include cupcakes, brownies, and pastries. She believed that by offering a variety of treats, she could cater to different customer preferences, thus increasing her customer base and revenue. But she also knew that this venture would not be without its challenges. It required careful planning, research, and execution.

She began by researching the market, understanding the demand for different types of pastries, and identifying her competitors. She also studied the ingredients, costs, and processes involved in baking these new products. After weeks of meticulous planning and preparation, she felt ready to introduce her new line of products.

As the first batch of cupcakes came out of the oven, Shreya could feel a mix of excitement and anticipation. She had put a lot of effort and resources into this new venture, and she hoped that her customers would love these new additions as much as they loved her cookies.

The response was overwhelming. The new line of treats was received with much enthusiasm, and the sales soared. The customers loved the variety and the unique flavours that each new product brought. The product line extension not only attracted new customers but also increased the frequency of visits from existing customers.

But as the business grew, so did the challenges. Managing a larger product line meant more complexity in operations, higher costs, and more time spent on quality control. However, Shreya was prepared. She had anticipated these challenges and planned accordingly. She hired more staff to manage the increased workload, invested in better equipment to maintain the quality of her products, and streamlined her operations to ensure efficiency.

The success of Sweet Delights is a testament to the power of product line extension. By understanding her customers and the market, Shreya was able to successfully expand her product line and grow her business. However, it also highlights the challenges that come with product line extension and the importance of careful planning and execution.

Shreya's story is a lesson for all businesses considering a product line extension. It shows that while product line extension can be a powerful tool for growth, it requires a deep understanding of the market, careful planning, and the ability to adapt to new challenges.

And so, the aroma of freshly baked cookies, cupcakes, and pastries continues to waft through the streets of Kolhapur, attracting customers far and wide to the little bakery called Sweet Delights. As for Shreya, she continues to innovate, always looking for new ways to delight her customers and grow her business.

GLOBALISATION

As the pages of our business case studies continue to unfold, we delve into the fascinating realm of globalisation, a phenomenon that has undeniably shaped the way businesses operate today. This chapter aims to walk you through the intricacies of globalisation and its impact, with an emphasis on real-life case studies that demonstrate its profound influence on business strategies, operations, and success.

Imagine a tapestry, vast and intricate. Each thread represents a different nation, as well as its businesses and economies. As the threads interweave, they form a complex pattern - this is globalisation. It is the process by which businesses or other organisations develop international influence or start operating on an international scale, weaving a network of worldwide interconnectivity and interdependence.

One cannot discuss globalisation without mentioning the case of Apple Inc. Once a small startup in the heart of Silicon

Valley, Apple has become a global powerhouse with a supply chain stretching across various continents. The company sources components from Japan, assembles products in China, holds its design and marketing teams in the USA, and sells its products worldwide. This case exemplifies how businesses can leverage globalisation, using the strengths of different regions to create a superior product.

However, globalisation is not just about multinational corporations. It's also about small businesses, like the local artisan who sells handmade crafts on Etsy to international customers. This global market access, made possible by the internet and international shipping, allows small businesses to reach customers beyond their local markets, contributing to the economic tapestry of globalisation.

Globalisation also fosters innovation and competition. Consider Spotify, a Swedish company that revolutionised the music industry with its streaming service. By operating globally, Spotify not only gained access to millions of listeners worldwide but also pushed other music providers to innovate, leading to a dynamic and competitive industry.

Yet, globalisation is not without its challenges. For instance, Starbucks' expansion into the Australian market serves as a cautionary tale. Despite its global brand recognition, Starbucks struggled to resonate with Australian consumers, who favoured local coffee shops. This case study underscores the importance of understanding local cultures and tastes in a global market.

Furthermore, globalisation can also lead to increased competition, as seen in the case of Kodak. Once a leader in photographic film, Kodak failed to adapt to the digital revolution, a global trend. The rise of companies like Sony and Canon in the digital space led to Kodak's eventual bankruptcy.

The case studies in this chapter offer an understanding of how globalisation impacts businesses. They illustrate how businesses can harness the power of globalisation to access new markets, source materials, and foster competition and innovation. At the same time, they also highlight the importance of adapting to local markets and staying competitive in a global arena.

In conclusion, globalisation, with all its opportunities and challenges, is a key factor shaping businesses today. As the threads of the tapestry continue to interweave, businesses must learn to adapt, innovate and thrive. The case studies presented herein provide valuable insights into navigating the complex, dynamic, and exciting world of globalisation.

ACQUISITIONS AND MERGERS

In the dynamic landscape of business, companies are always seeking ways to expand their reach, diversify their portfolio, or enhance their competitive advantage. Two strategies often employed are acquisitions and mergers. While both involve the combination of two entities, they are distinct in their specifics and outcomes, and they present unique case studies in the world of business.

Take, for example, the iconic merger between Disney and Pixar. Prior to their union, Disney was struggling with its animation department, while Pixar was rising as a formidable force in the industry. Their merger in 2006 turned the tables dramatically. Disney benefited from Pixar's creative genius, and Pixar gained access to Disney's extensive distribution network and vast resources. It was a win-win situation that resulted in a series of successful films and a rejuvenated Disney brand. This case study exemplifies how a well-executed merger can breathe new life into established companies and catalyse innovation.

On the other hand, we have the acquisition of Instagram by Facebook. Instagram, a burgeoning social media platform, was purchased by Facebook in 2012. While some feared that Facebook would stifle Instagram's innovation, the opposite occurred. Facebook allowed Instagram to operate independently, preserving its unique culture and user experience. Meanwhile, Instagram benefited from Facebook's resources and user base, propelling its growth exponentially. This acquisition case study demonstrates how strategic purchases can enhance a company's offerings and strengthen its market position.

However, not all mergers and acquisitions (M&As) lead to success. Consider the merger between AOL and Time Warner. Hailed as a revolutionary deal that would combine old and new media, it instead became one of the most infamous failures in business history. The cultures of the two companies clashed, their business models were incompatible, and the anticipated synergies never materialised. The merger resulted in massive financial losses and was eventually dissolved. This case study underscores the importance of due diligence, compatibility, and strategic planning in M&As.

A more recent acquisition that faced significant challenges was Amazon's purchase of Whole Foods. Amazon, a tech giant known for its e-commerce prowess, bought Whole Foods, a high-end grocery chain, in a move that shocked the industry. While the acquisition promised to revolutionise grocery shopping by integrating online and offline experiences, it faced considerable hurdles, from cultural differences to logistical issues. Nevertheless, it also opened up new opportunities for both companies, such as the expansion of Amazon's grocery delivery service. This case study illustrates how acquisitions can propel companies into new markets, as well as the difficulties inherent in integrating different business models and cultures.

In conclusion, acquisitions and mergers are powerful tools that can transform businesses for better or worse. They can foster innovation, expand market reach, and strengthen competitive advantage. However, they also come with risks and challenges, from cultural clashes to logistical hurdles. Therefore, they require careful planning, strategic execution, and constant monitoring. The case studies of Disney-Pixar, Facebook-Instagram, AOL-Time Warner, and Amazon-Whole Foods provide valuable lessons in the potentials and pitfalls of M&As, illuminating the complexities of this business strategy.

Chapter 6
MARKETING AND BRANDING

BRAND IDENTITY

As the first rays of dawn appeared on the horizon, Vinod, the owner of a small but ambitious startup, sat at his desk, engrossed in thought. He was contemplating the core principles that would define his business. He was envisioning something that would not only distinguish his company from the competition but also create a bond with his customers. In essence, he was contemplating the creation of a brand identity.

The concept of brand identity, he realised, was not just about a catchy name or a compelling logo. It was, in fact, the very soul of his business, the core essence that would be communicated to his customers and the world at large. It was a promise of what his company stood for, what it aimed to deliver, and the experience it intended to provide.

Delving deeper into the concept, Vinod understood that brand identity was a potent tool that could shape perception and influence behaviour. It was a combination of tangible elements like the company's name, logo, and design, as well as intangible aspects such as the company's vision, values, and personality. Together, these elements created a unique image in the minds of the customers, differentiating the company in the crowded marketplace.

To illustrate his understanding, he thought of Apple Inc., a brand that had managed to carve a unique identity for itself. Apple's brand identity was not just about its iconic logo or its sleek product design. It was about innovation, simplicity, and sophistication. It was about the promise of providing cutting-edge technology in a user-friendly format. This strong brand identity not only helped Apple differentiate itself but also created a loyal customer base that saw value in being associated with the brand.

However, Vinod realised that creating a strong brand identity was not an easy task. It required a deep understanding of the company's mission, vision, and values, as well as its target audience. It required consistency in communication and a commitment to delivering on the promises made. It required the ability to adapt and evolve while staying true to the core essence of the brand.

He thought of Starbucks, a brand that had managed to evolve its brand identity over the years. Starting as a single coffee shop in Seattle, Starbucks has grown into a global brand synonymous with a unique coffee-drinking experience. The brand had evolved, adapting to different cultures and trends, but had remained true to its core promise of providing a third place between home and work.

As he sat there, the first rays of dawn giving way to the morning light, Vinod felt a sense of clarity. He realised that the journey towards creating a strong brand identity for his startup would be challenging. But it was a journey he was ready to embark upon, a journey that would define the future of his business.

In the end, he understood that brand identity was not just about making a mark. It was about making a difference. It was about creating an entity that resonated with the customers, an entity that, in its own unique way, added value to their lives. As the sun rose higher in the sky, Vinod, with renewed vigour and determination, set out on this exciting journey of defining his brand identity.

MARKETING STRATEGIES

In the bustling world of business, companies are often faced with the challenge of standing out amidst a sea of competitors. A significant aspect of this challenge lies in the realm of marketing, the art of promoting and selling products or services. The most successful businesses have, over time, employed unique and effective marketing strategies, turning the tide in their favour. Our exploration of these case studies will uncover the magic behind these strategies.

Consider the case of Apple Inc., a technological titan that has revolutionised the industry with its innovative products. Their marketing strategy is a tapestry of simplicity, innovation, and exclusivity woven meticulously into a powerful brand image. The company's iconic product launches and keynote addresses have a theatrical flair that stirs anticipation and excitement among consumers, creating an aura of desirability around their products. This strategy has not only helped Apple command premium prices for its products but also fostered a loyal customer base that eagerly awaits each new release.

On the other hand, we have Nike, a global sportswear powerhouse. Their marketing strategy is deeply rooted in the power of storytelling and emotional connection. Nike's advertisements often feature inspiring stories of athletes overcoming adversity, tying their brand to the universal themes of perseverance and triumph. This strategy has allowed Nike to transcend beyond just selling sportswear to selling a mindset, making it a beloved brand worldwide.

Next, let's examine the case of Coca-Cola, a brand synonymous with refreshment. Coca-Cola's marketing strategy revolves around creating memorable experiences. From its iconic Christmas commercials to the 'Share a Coke' campaign, where bottles were personalised with popular names, Coca-Cola has consistently used its marketing to evoke feelings of happiness and togetherness. This strategy has helped Coca-Cola to cement its position as a global leader in the beverage industry.

Tesla Inc., the renowned electric vehicle manufacturer, offers another interesting case study. Their marketing strategy is a stark departure from traditional methods. Tesla does not invest in advertising. Instead, it leverages the power of word-of-mouth and social media, fuelled by its charismatic CEO, Elon Musk. This unconventional approach has worked wonders for Tesla, helping it garner a cult-like following and becoming a leader in the electric vehicle market.

Finally, let's delve into the strategy of McDonald's, a fast-food giant. McDonald's marketing strategy hinges on the concept of consistency and familiarity. From its universally recognised golden arches to its consistent menu, McDonald's offers a familiar experience to customers worldwide. This strategy has enabled McDonald's to build a strong global presence and become a household name.

In conclusion, these case studies underscore the significance of a well-crafted marketing strategy. Whether it's Apple's exclusivity, Nike's emotional storytelling, Coca-Cola's memorable experiences, Tesla's word-of-mouth, or McDonald's consistency, each strategy is unique and tailored to the brand's identity and target audience. These strategies have not only driven sales but also shaped the brand's image, proving how powerful a tool marketing can be in the world of business.

DIGITAL MARKETING

In the bustling market of modern business, a tale of transformation unfolded. The protagonist of this story was a small, family-owned business named "Bakery." They had been serving their local community with delicious pastries and bread since 1990. However, with the dawn of the digital age, the once-thriving bakery was struggling to keep pace with the changing times. This is where our journey into the world of digital marketing begins.

Bakery, known for its old-world charm and mouth-watering recipes, was losing business to larger, more tech-savvy competitors. Their traditional methods of advertising, such as flyers, billboards, and local newspaper ads, were no longer as effective. The owners, the family, knew they had to change their approach to stay afloat, and that's when they decided to embrace digital marketing.

The first step in their digital marketing journey was to establish an online presence. They hired a web designer to create a user-friendly website showcasing their products and telling the story of their brand. The website also provided customers with the ability to place orders online, a feature that was becoming increasingly popular in the bakery business.

To increase their visibility, they also created profiles on several social media platforms. The Bakery took to platforms like Instagram and Facebook, where they shared enticing photos of their pastries and bread, news about special offers, and stories from behind the scenes. They discovered the power of hashtags and learned how to use these to increase their reach. They also started interacting with their customers online, responding to comments and messages, which further helped to humanise their brand.

Investing in search engine optimisation (SEO) was another key aspect of their digital marketing strategy. They wanted to ensure that when potential customers searched for bakeries in their area, the Bakery would be among the top results. They hired an SEO expert who helped them optimise their website with relevant keywords and backlinks to improve their search engine rankings.

Email marketing was another tool they utilised. They started collecting email addresses from their customers, promising to keep them updated about new products, special offers, and events. These emails not only helped in retaining their existing customers but also attracted new ones.

Their efforts began to pay off. People started discovering Bakery online. The website and social media profiles drove a significant increase in their sales. Their customer base started growing, not just locally but from neighbouring towns and cities as well. The engagement they received on their social media posts helped them understand their customers better and tailor their offerings accordingly.

Digital marketing had breathed new life into the Bakery. It helped them compete with larger businesses and reach a wider audience. It provided them with tools to understand their customers better and serve them more effectively. The Bakery realised that digital marketing was not just about selling products online; it was about building relationships with their customers and creating an online community around their brand.

This is the power of digital marketing. It can transform a small, struggling business into a thriving, competitive entity. It levels the playing field, allowing smaller businesses to compete with larger ones. Digital marketing is not just a trend but a necessity in today's digital age. The story of Bakery serves as a testament to this.

In the world of business, digital marketing is the hero that every company needs. And like every hero's journey, it starts with a single step: the decision to embrace the digital world. For Bakery, this decision was the beginning of a new chapter in their business, one that led them to success in the digital age.

CUSTOMER RELATIONSHIP MANAGEMENT

In the thriving hub of the business world, where competition is fierce and the pace of innovation is relentless, maintaining a strong bond with customers is paramount. This pivotal aspect of business success is beautifully illustrated through an exploration of customer relationship management (CRM), a strategic approach that has revolutionised the way businesses interact with their customers.

Picture a bustling café in the heart of a city, where the aroma of freshly ground coffee beans fills the air. The café prides itself on creating a personalised experience for each customer. The barista, with a warm smile, greets every customer by name, remembers their favourite blend of coffee, and even recalls small details from previous conversations. This café has mastered the art of CRM at a micro level. But how does this translate to larger businesses, where the customer base is in the thousands or even millions?

Let's turn our attention to a company that has made headlines with its innovative approach to CRM - Amazon. The online retail giant has harnessed the power of technology to create a personalised shopping experience for each of its millions of customers. Their CRM strategy is built around a sophisticated algorithm that tracks customer behaviour, including their browsing history, purchase history, and feedback. This data is then used to recommend products that align with the customer's interests and needs. It's like having a personal shopper who knows your tastes perfectly and can recommend products you'll love.

The brilliance of Amazon's CRM strategy lies not only in its personalisation but also in its consistency. No matter which device a customer uses to access Amazon, their experience is seamless. Their shopping cart, wish list, and recommended products are synchronised across all devices, creating a smooth, consistent experience that builds trust and loyalty.

However, CRM isn't just about selling more products. It's also about providing exceptional customer service. When a customer has a problem or a question, how a company responds can make or break their relationship. Let's look at Zappos, an online shoe retailer known for its extraordinary customer service. Zappos has a 365-day return policy and provides free shipping both ways, making online shopping virtually risk-free for customers. Their customer service representatives are empowered to do whatever it takes to make customers happy, even if it means bending the rules occasionally. This commitment to customer satisfaction has earned Zappos a loyal customer base and a reputation for excellence in customer service.

In both of these case studies, the common thread is an unwavering focus on the customer. CRM is not a one-size-fits-all solution; it must be tailored to the needs and preferences of a company's specific customer base. It requires a deep understanding of who the customers are, what they want, and how the company can deliver it in a way that not only meets but exceeds their expectations.

In the end, CRM is about building relationships. Just like the barista at the café who knows each customer by name, businesses must strive to understand and connect with their customers on a personal level. In the fast-paced, competitive world of business, relationships set a company apart.

Chapter 7

FINANCIAL MANAGEMENT

FUNDING AND INVESTMENT

As our journey into the labyrinth of business case studies unfolds, we take a turn into a corridor that leads us to the heart of any business endeavour - the realm of funding and investment. This is an arena where dreams are either brought to life or crushed under the weight of financial realities. It's a world that, while complex, can be navigated successfully with the right knowledge and strategies.

We begin our exploration with the tale of a budding entrepreneur, Nikhil, who had a vision for a tech startup that could revolutionise the industry. Nikhil had the technical skills, the innovative ideas, and the passion to make it all happen. But he lacked one crucial thing - the capital to get his venture off the ground. This is a predicament many entrepreneurs find themselves in, and it's a hurdle that can seem insurmountable.

Enter the world of angel investors and venture capitalists. These are the individuals and entities willing to take a chance on promising startups in exchange for a stake in the company. Nikhil took the plunge and pitched his idea to numerous potential investors. It was an arduous process, one filled with countless rejections and sleepless nights. But perseverance paid off when he finally secured the funding needed to bring his vision to life.

This story underscores the importance of investment in the business world. It's the lifeblood that allows companies to grow, innovate, and ultimately succeed. Without it, even the most brilliant ideas can wither on the vine. But securing investment is no easy feat. It requires a compelling business case, a sound strategy, and, often, a healthy dose of tenacity.

Our journey then takes us to the other side of the table - to the world of the investors themselves. We delve into the case of Sanskrit, a seasoned venture capitalist with a keen eye for identifying promising startups. Sanskrit's success hinges on her ability to accurately assess the potential of a business and make calculated decisions about where to invest her funds.

We follow Sanskrit as she navigates through a sea of pitches, scrutinises business plans, and grapples with the inherent uncertainty that comes with investing in startups. It's a high-stakes game, one where the risks are as great as the potential rewards. Through Sanskrit's story, we gain insights into the complexities and nuances of making investment decisions.

The realm of funding and investment is a crucial part of the business ecosystem. It's a dynamic, often challenging environment that can make or break a business venture. But as our journey through this corridor has shown, with the right strategies, knowledge, and a bit of persistence, it's a realm that can be successfully navigated.

In the end, the stories of Nikhil and Sanskrit serve as powerful illustrations of the intricacies of funding and investment. They provide valuable lessons for both entrepreneurs seeking capital and investors looking for their next big success story. As we continue our journey through the world of business case studies, we carry with us the insights gleaned from this corridor, ready to apply them to the challenges and opportunities that lie ahead.

CASH FLOW MANAGEMENT

In the bustling heart of New Delhi, nestled among towering skyscrapers, a small but successful tech startup was teetering on the edge of disaster. It wasn't due to a lack of customers or a faulty product. The problem was cash flow. Despite a seemingly successful operation, the company was grappling with managing its cash flow, a common issue for many businesses, which ultimately makes or breaks their survival.

The company, let's call it TechI, had a promising product - a unique software solution that was rapidly gaining popularity. Success was at their fingertips, but so was financial ruin. The paradox was glaring. The company had a robust sales pipeline, a growing list of customers, and a product that was in demand. But their bank account told a different story. It was steadily dwindling, threatening to pull the rug from under their feet.

The heart of the issue was that TechI was not receiving payments from their customers quickly enough to cover their immediate expenses. They had to pay their employees, rent, utilities, and vendors, but the cash coming in from their customers was not keeping pace. This led to a negative cash flow, a situation where the cash outflows exceeded the cash inflows.

To address this, TechI needed to implement effective cash flow management strategies. The CEO, a dynamic and forward-thinking leader, decided to revisit their payment terms with customers. They began offering discounts to customers who paid their invoices early. This enticed more customers to pay promptly, thereby improving the cash flow.

Simultaneously, they negotiated with their vendors for extended payment terms. This gave them more time to pay their bills without incurring late fees or damaging their relationships with the vendors. These adjustments helped to ease the cash flow pressure and allowed the company to continue operating smoothly.

But the CEO knew that these measures were only a band-aid solution. They needed a more comprehensive approach to cash flow management. So, they invested in cash flow management software. This tool provided them with real-time visibility into their cash flow. It helped them forecast their cash inflows and outflows, allowing them to plan and manage their cash resources better.

TechI also prioritised building a cash reserve. They understood that having a cash cushion could provide them with the financial stability they needed during unforeseen circumstances. They started setting aside a certain percentage of their revenue into a separate account, gradually building a substantial cash reserve.

As TechI implemented these strategies, they began to see a significant improvement in their cash flow situation. Their bank account was no longer dwindling. They had the funds to cover their expenses and invest in growth initiatives. The company was finally on stable financial ground.

This story of TechI underscores the importance of cash flow management in business. It shows that even a successful company can face financial difficulties if they do not effectively manage their cash flow. Cash flow management is not just about survival but also about creating opportunities for growth and expansion. It's a crucial aspect that should never be overlooked in the pursuit of business success.

PROFIT MAXIMISATION

In the vast landscape of commerce and industry, the pursuit of profit maximisation has always been a beacon guiding businesses towards their ultimate destination. This chapter delves into the intricate world of profit maximisation, a concept that forms the very foundation of all successful business ventures.

Imagine a ship sailing across the vast ocean with the captain at the helm, eyes fixed on the horizon, constantly adjusting the course to ensure the ship stays on the right path. The pursuit of profit in a business is akin to this journey. The captain, in this case, is the business owner or the management team, the ship represents the business entity, and the ocean symbolises the market with its unpredictable and ever-changing conditions. The horizon, of course, signifies the ultimate goal — profit maximisation.

To start, let's understand what profit maximisation truly means. At its core, it refers to a strategic business decision-making process aimed at achieving the highest possible profit with the least amount of risk. It is a delicate balancing act between managing costs, setting competitive prices, and ensuring customer satisfaction.

Consider the case of a popular electronics company. The management needs to make strategic decisions regarding the production of their devices. They must consider the cost of raw materials, labour, and other overhead expenses. If they price their products too high, they risk alienating customers and losing market share. If they price too low, they might not cover their costs or achieve their desired profit margin.

Profit maximisation is not just about increasing revenue; it's also about managing and reducing costs. Businesses often overlook this aspect, focusing solely on sales and revenue. However, even the most successful companies can face financial difficulties if they do not manage their costs effectively.

For instance, a restaurant may be popular and always full, but if the cost of ingredients, labour, rent, and other overheads are not managed properly, it could still end up in financial distress. Therefore, effective cost management is a critical component of profit maximisation.

Another significant aspect is risk management. Businesses operate in a dynamic environment with numerous uncertainties. Market conditions, customer preferences, technological advancements, and regulatory changes are just a few examples of factors that can affect a business's profitability. Therefore, part of maximising profit involves anticipating these risks and implementing strategies to mitigate them.

Take the case of a clothing retailer that sources materials from overseas. A sudden increase in import tariffs or a disruption in supply chains could significantly impact the cost of goods and, consequently, profitability. Therefore, the retailer might diversify its supply sources or negotiate better deals with suppliers as a risk mitigation strategy.

Profit maximisation also requires businesses to constantly innovate and adapt to changing market conditions. This might involve investing in new technologies, exploring new markets, diversifying product offerings, or improving customer service.

In conclusion, profit maximisation is a complex process that requires strategic planning, effective cost management, risk mitigation, and continuous innovation. It is the compass that guides businesses through the turbulent seas of the market, helping them navigate towards their ultimate goal of achieving the highest possible profit.

This chapter has provided a broad overview of the concept of profit maximisation. The subsequent sections will delve deeper into each component, providing case studies to illustrate how businesses have successfully implemented these strategies.

FINANCIAL RISK MANAGEMENT

In the dynamic landscape of business, there was one aspect that remained a constant challenge - managing financial risk. It was a game of strategy, one that required a keen eye and a sharp mind. The stakes were high, and the consequences of missteps were severe, but the rewards for successful navigation were immense.

In the bustling city of Mumbai, a company named TechS had made a name for itself. It was an ambitious startup that had quickly risen to prominence in the tech industry. However, with rapid growth came the inevitable risks, particularly on the financial front. The company's CFO, a seasoned veteran named Rishi, was tasked with the critical responsibility of managing these risks.

Rishi's day began with a review of the financial markets. He looked at the trends, the fluctuations, the ups and downs. He analysed the patterns, predicting potential shifts and preparing for possible challenges. He had to be proactive, always one step ahead, always ready for the unexpected.

Rishi also had to consider the company's internal financial situation. He had to ensure that the company's resources were being used efficiently and effectively. This required careful budgeting, diligent tracking of expenses, and strategic allocation of funds. He had to balance the company's immediate needs with its long-term goals, a task that required both prudence and foresight.

Another critical aspect of Rishi's role was risk assessment. He had to identify potential threats to the company's financial stability and develop strategies to mitigate them. This could involve anything from diversifying the company's investments to securing insurance coverage. It was a delicate balancing act, one that required a deep understanding of both the company's operations and the broader business environment.

In the world of financial risk management, communication is key. Rishi had to regularly report to the company's board of directors, keeping them informed about the company's financial status and the risks it was facing. He had to be transparent, honest, and clear, ensuring that the board had all the information it needed to make informed decisions.

Rishi also had to communicate with the company's employees. He had to ensure that they understood the company's financial situation and the steps being taken to manage risk. This required a knack for explaining complex financial concepts in a way that was easy to understand, a skill that Rishi had honed over the years.

Despite the challenges, Rishi found his work immensely rewarding. He knew that his efforts were crucial to the company's success and that he was playing a key role in steering the company towards a secure and prosperous future. He understood that financial risk management was not just about numbers and figures but about safeguarding the company's vision, its mission, and its very essence.

In the fast-paced, high-stakes world of business, companies like TechS relied on the expertise and acumen of professionals like Rishi. They were the unsung heroes, the guardians of financial stability. They were the ones who navigated the turbulent seas of risk, charting a course towards success.

This, then, was the world of financial risk management - a world of strategy, analysis, and foresight. A world where the stakes were high, but the rewards were even higher. A world that was at the very heart of the business, shaping its present and moulding its future.

Chapter 8

HUMAN RESOURCE MANAGEMENT

RECRUITMENT AND SELECTION

In the bustling heart of a thriving organisation, the tale of its success is often etched in the strength and capabilities of its workforce. The story of how these individuals came to be a part of the organisation, their recruitment and selection, is a critical chapter in the grand narrative of any business.

Imagine a dynamic business entity; let's call it 'Company X'. Company X was on a rapid growth trajectory spurred by a unique business model and an innovative product. However, to maintain this meteoric rise, it needed a fuel of its own - a talented and dedicated workforce. The story of how Company X went about recruiting and selecting its team is one of strategy, foresight, and careful execution.

The recruitment tale commenced with Company X identifying its needs. The management team meticulously mapped out the skills, qualifications, and experience required for each role. They took into account not just the immediate needs of the organisation but also its future aspirations. Recognising the fact that the right people could propel the company to new heights, they left no stone unturned in outlining the perfect candidate profiles.

Next came the search. Company X scoured multiple platforms, from job portals and recruitment agencies to social media and university job fairs. It was a strategic move aimed at casting a wide net to attract diverse talents. The company also incentivised its existing employees to refer potential candidates, thereby leveraging their networks.

However, the real challenge lies in the selection process. Company X was aware that the right hire was not just about the right skills but also about the right fit. It designed a multi-stage interview process to assess the candidates. The process included not just technical rounds to evaluate the skills but also behavioural interviews to understand the candidate's cultural fit, work ethic, and potential for growth.

But the tale doesn't end with the job offer. Company X made efforts to engage with the candidates throughout the process. It ensured that the candidates had a positive experience, regardless of the outcome of their application. This was not just about filling a position; it was about building a brand reputation, about letting the world know that Company X was an employer of choice.

In the end, Company X's recruitment and selection process became a cornerstone of its success. The company was able to build a team of dedicated, skilled, and motivated individuals who were not just employees but brand ambassadors. They were the ones who drove the company's growth, who innovated, who helped Company X navigate through challenges and seize opportunities.

Thus, the story of recruitment and selection is not just about filling up vacancies. It is about strategic planning, understanding the business needs, attracting the right talent, and making the right choice. It is an ongoing narrative that shapes the destiny of the organisation. It is a tale that underscores the fact that the people make the business and that the right people can take the business to unparalleled heights.

TRAINING AND DEVELOPMENT

In the bustling world of commerce, a thriving company was navigating its way through the challenges of the market. It was a company renowned for its exceptional services and products. However, the management was well aware that they owed their success not only to their innovative solutions but also to the people who worked tirelessly behind the scenes. They knew that their employees were their most valuable asset, and they were committed to investing in their growth.

The company recognised that the landscape of business was ever-changing. To stay ahead, they needed to constantly adapt and evolve. They understood that the key to adaptation was not only in the development of new products and services but also in the continuous training and development of their workforce.

They began by assessing the current skills and knowledge of their employees. They wanted to identify the areas where their employees excelled and the areas they needed to improve. The management believed that by understanding their employees' strengths and weaknesses, they could tailor the training to their specific needs.

The company then designed a comprehensive training programme. It was not just a series of lectures or presentations. Instead, it was a carefully planned journey that aimed to equip their employees with the latest tools and techniques in their field. The programme was interactive and engaging, allowing the employees to learn by doing. It was a mixture of theoretical knowledge and practical applications, ensuring that the employees could immediately apply what they learned.

Moreover, the company also focuses on the personal development of its employees. They understood that each employee was unique, with their own set of skills, interests, and aspirations. They provided opportunities for their employees to pursue their passions, to explore new areas, and to grow as individuals. They offered mentorship programmes, where experienced professionals guided the less experienced ones. They also provided resources for self-learning, encouraging their employees to take charge of their own development.

The company also recognised the importance of feedback in the process of training and development. They established a system where employees could regularly receive constructive feedback on their performance. This allowed the employees to understand their progress, to identify their areas of improvement, and to continuously strive for excellence.

The results were astounding. The employees were more motivated and engaged. They were more competent and confident in their roles. They were able to adapt better to the changes in the market, contributing to the company's resilience and growth.

The company's commitment to training and development also had a significant impact on its reputation. It attracted talented individuals who were eager to work in a company that valued their growth. It also enhanced their relationship with their clients, who appreciated the company's dedication to excellence.

This case study illustrates the power of training and development in business. It shows that investing in the growth of employees is not just a moral obligation but also a strategic move. It is a testament that when a company values its people, the people will value the company. And when the people value the company, the company thrives.

EMPLOYEE RETENTION

In the bustling world of corporate affairs, a successful company has a secret weapon, a key driving force that propels it towards its goals. This crucial element is none other than its employees. The intricate web of business operations is held together by the hard work and dedication of these individuals. Hence, it becomes imperative for companies to hold on to their valuable employees, a concept known as employee retention.

In the case of TT Inc., a multinational technology company, the importance of employee retention was learned the hard way. Known for its innovative products and services, the company was a market leader in its sector. However, the company began to witness an alarming trend. Its talented workforce was leaving, moving on to greener pastures, leaving behind a void that was hard to fill.

The company's leadership was left in a state of confusion and concern. They had always prided themselves on their competitive salaries and benefits package. So, why were their employees leaving? A deep dive into the issue revealed that while the company was indeed providing competitive monetary benefits, it was failing to meet the employees' non-monetary needs. The work environment was stressful, and the employees felt overworked and underappreciated. The lack of work-life balance and recognition was driving the employees away.

It was a wake-up call for TT Inc. The company realised that employee retention was not merely about competitive salaries but also about creating a nurturing work environment.

It undertook a series of measures to address the issue. Flexible work hours, remote working options, recognition programmes, and employee wellness initiatives were introduced. The company also started conducting regular surveys to gauge employee satisfaction and to identify areas of improvement.

The results were not immediate, but gradually, the company began to see a change. Employee turnover rates started to decrease, and the company was able to retain its talented workforce. More importantly, the employees felt valued and appreciated, leading to increased productivity and job satisfaction.

The case of TT Inc. serves as a valuable lesson in the importance of employee retention. It showcases that employees are not merely resources but the backbone of a company. They need to be nurtured, appreciated, and given the right environment to flourish.

In the world of business, companies often focus on acquiring new customers to drive growth. However, they forget that retaining existing employees is just as important, if not more. A high employee turnover rate can be detrimental to a company's growth and reputation. It can lead to a loss of valuable knowledge and skills, increased recruitment costs, and decreased productivity and morale among remaining employees.

In conclusion, employee retention is not a one-time effort but an ongoing process. It requires a holistic approach that caters to the various needs of the employees. Competitive salaries, a nurturing work environment, recognition, and opportunities for growth and development are all crucial components of employee retention. As the case of TT Inc. illustrates, a company that succeeds in retaining its employees is a company that is on the path to success.

CONFLICT RESOLUTION

The tension was palpable as the boardroom door swung shut. Two of the company's most influential senior executives, Sanskrit and Ashtami, were locked in a fierce disagreement that had been brewing for weeks. The focal point was the company's strategic direction, and their contrasting viewpoints had polarised the rest of the team. The situation was a classic example of a conflict that needed resolution, a vital aspect of business management that often decides the fate of organisations.

Sanskrit, the company's Chief Financial Officer, was a staunch advocate for cost-cutting and efficiency. She believed in tight controls, lean operations, and a strong focus on financial metrics. She was convinced that this was the only way to ensure the company's survival in an increasingly competitive market.

On the other hand, Ashtami, the Chief Marketing Officer, was a firm believer in investment and growth. She argued that the company needed to invest heavily in marketing and innovation to differentiate itself and capture new market segments. To her, Sanskrit's cost-cutting approach was short-sighted and threatened the company's long-term growth potential.

The conflict had reached a point where it was affecting team morale and productivity. Meetings were becoming battlegrounds, and the rest of the team felt caught in the crossfire. It was clear that this conflict needed resolution and fast.

The CEO, recognising the gravity of the situation, decided to intervene. He invited both Sanskrit and Ashtami to a private meeting to discuss their differences. He started by acknowledging the value of their perspectives and emphasising the importance of their roles in the company. He made it clear that their conflict was not about who was right or wrong but about finding the best way forward for the company.

The CEO then facilitated a discussion where Sanskrit and Ashtami were encouraged to express their viewpoints openly while listening to each other's perspectives. He emphasised the importance of empathy in understanding each other's viewpoints and finding common ground.

As the discussion progressed, it became clear that both Sanskrit and Ashtami had the company's best interests at heart. They both agreed on the need for fiscal responsibility and growth but differed on how to achieve these goals. This realisation helped to defuse the tension and opened up the possibility of compromise.

The CEO proposed a balanced approach that incorporated both cost-efficiency and strategic investment. He suggested that some cost-cutting measures could be implemented, but not at the expense of growth initiatives. Similarly, investments in marketing and innovation would be made, but with a keen eye on return on investment.

Sanskrit and Ashtami, seeing the wisdom in this balanced approach, agreed to put their differences aside and work together for the benefit of the company. The rest of the team, witnessing this resolution, felt a sense of relief and renewed motivation.

In conclusion, conflict resolution in business is not just about resolving disagreements. It's about facilitating open communication, fostering understanding, and finding a path that aligns with the organisation's goals. By doing so, companies can turn conflicts into opportunities for growth and innovation.

Chapter 9
INNOVATION AND TECHNOLOGY

ADOPTING TECHNOLOGY

In the bustling heart of Mumbai, a small but ambitious startup was making waves. HTech, a budding tech company, was poised on the brink of an innovative leap. They had developed a state-of-the-art software solution that could streamline business operations like never before. However, the challenge lay in introducing this technological marvel to the market and convincing businesses to adopt it. This was the critical juncture where HTech found itself.

The company's CEO, a dynamic woman named Namrata, knew the importance of strategic implementation. She was aware that the key to successful adoption lay in understanding the needs and apprehensions of potential clients. She also knew that the value of technology had to be communicated effectively to potential adopters. With this in mind, Namrata and her team began working on a comprehensive adoption strategy.

Firstly, they conducted extensive market research to understand the potential users' pain points, their current systems, and where their new software could fit in. They found that while businesses understood the need for technological advancement, many were apprehensive about the transition process. They worried about the cost, the time it would take, and the potential disruption to their existing operations.

With this insight, HTech focused on developing a seamless onboarding process. They designed a system that would allow businesses to transition gradually, ensuring minimal disruption to their operations. They also offered comprehensive training and support, aiming to make the shift as smooth as possible.

Simultaneously, HTech also worked on communicating the value of their software. They highlighted its efficiency, cost-effectiveness, and the competitive advantage it would provide. They used case studies, demonstrations, and testimonials to prove its effectiveness.

Moreover, Namrata understood the importance of securing buy-in from all levels of a potential client's organisation. She knew that for successful technology adoption, it wasn't enough to convince just the top management. The end-users, the employees who would be working with the software daily, also needed to see its value. Thus, HTech's marketing and training efforts targeted not just decision-makers but also end-users.

HTech's strategy seemed to be working. Businesses were showing interest, and a few even signed up for trials. However, Namrata knew that this was just the beginning. For widespread technology adoption, they needed to continually support their clients, evolve based on their feedback, and prove that their software was not just a fancy tool but a game-changing solution.

One of the first businesses to adopt HTech's software was a mid-sized retail company. The transition wasn't without hiccups, but HTech's support team was always on hand to assist. Over time, the company began to see the software's value. Their operations became smoother, their costs reduced, and their decision-making process became more data-driven. Satisfied with the results, they became a long-term client, providing HTech with a success story to share with potential adopters.

HTech's journey is a testament to the challenges and strategies involved in technology adoption. It underlines the importance of understanding potential adopters' needs, developing a user-friendly onboarding process, effectively communicating the technology's value, and securing buy-in from all levels of an organisation. As businesses continue to navigate the digital age, these lessons remain crucial.

INNOVATION IN BUSINESS

The essence of every successful business lies in its ability to innovate and adapt to the changing market dynamics. The narrative of innovation in business is a tapestry woven with threads of creativity, risk-taking, and a relentless pursuit of growth. In the business landscape, it is the innovators who often rewrite the rules of the game, leaving an indelible mark on the industry and setting new benchmarks for others to follow.

The story of Apple Inc., under the visionary leadership of Steve Jobs, serves as a compelling case study in innovation. The company's journey from a garage startup to a global tech giant is a testament to the power of disruptive innovation. Apple didn't just create products; they revolutionised entire markets, from personal computing with the Mac to music distribution with the iPod and iTunes and, later, mobile technology with the iPhone. Apple's innovative approach has not only been about creating new products but also about redefining existing ones, thereby shaping consumer behaviour and expectations.

Similarly, Amazon's narrative, led by Jeff Bezos, underscores the significance of continuous innovation in business. Amazon transformed from an online bookstore into a global e-commerce and technology powerhouse. The company's innovative strategies, such as the introduction of Amazon Prime, a membership programme offering free shipping and access to digital media, and Amazon Web Services, a highly profitable cloud computing platform, have been instrumental in its meteoric rise. Amazon's culture of innovation is rooted in its willingness to experiment, learn from failures, and relentlessly focus on customer needs.

However, innovation is not limited to tech giants. Small and medium enterprises (SMEs) also play a pivotal role in driving innovation. A case in point is Patagonia, an outdoor clothing company that has consistently been at the forefront of environmental and social responsibility. The company's innovative business model - pledging 1% of sales to the preservation and restoration of the natural environment, encouraging customers to buy fewer products, and investing in sustainable materials and processes - has set it apart from its competitors. Patagonia's success illustrates that innovation can be as much about 'how' a company does business as it is about 'what' it does.

The narrative of innovation in business also highlights the importance of fostering a culture that encourages creativity and out-of-the-box thinking. Google's '20% time' policy, where employees can spend 20% of their time working on personal projects, has led to the development of some of its most successful products, such as Gmail and AdSense. This policy shows that innovation can be nurtured by creating an environment that values and promotes freedom, flexibility, and experimentation.

In conclusion, innovation in business is not a one-time event but a continuous process. It requires a mindset that embraces change, values creativity, and is not afraid to take calculated risks. The stories of Apple, Amazon, Patagonia, and Google underscore that innovation can take various forms - from disruptive products and services to innovative business models and cultures. These narratives serve as an inspiration for businesses across the spectrum to innovate, evolve, and create value in the ever-changing marketplace.

DIGITAL TRANSFORMATION

In the ever-evolving world of business, there came a time when the tides began to shift dramatically. It was as though a digital hurricane had swept over the landscape, reshaping it into something almost unrecognisable. This was the dawn of the digital transformation era.

Every business, be it a multi-billion-dollar corporation or a humble mom-and-pop shop, felt the tremors of this seismic shift. It was no longer enough to simply have a solid product or service offering. The digital age demands more. It demanded that businesses transform, not only in terms of technology but also in their mindset, culture, and operations.

Consider the case of Blockbuster, once a titan in the video rental industry. At its peak, Blockbuster was a household name, with a vast network of physical stores spread across continents. However, as the digital age ushered in, companies like Netflix began to offer a new, more convenient way to consume entertainment – streaming. Blockbuster, unable to adapt to this digital shift, eventually declared bankruptcy.

On the other end of the spectrum, there's the story of Domino's Pizza. In the early 2000s, Domino's was struggling. Their pizza was criticised for its quality, and their delivery service was not up to par. Recognising the need for change, Domino's decided to embrace digital transformation. They revamped their menu and invested heavily in technology to improve customer experience. Today, Domino's is known for its innovative digital initiatives, from online ordering and real-time pizza tracking to AI chatbots and drone deliveries. This digital transformation has helped Domino's become one of the leading pizza delivery companies in the world.

These contrasting tales of Blockbuster and Domino's illustrate the importance of digital transformation in today's business environment. It's not just about adopting the latest technologies; it's about maintaining a competitive edge. It's about understanding and meeting customer expectations in a digital world. It's about being agile, innovative, and ready to evolve with the times.

Digital transformation is a journey, not a destination. It requires a clear vision, strong leadership, and a willingness to take risks. It's about creating a digital-first culture, where technology is seen not as a threat but as an opportunity to enhance business performance and customer experience.

The process of digital transformation can be challenging. It may involve redefining business models, retraining staff, and reimagining customer interactions. But the potential rewards – increased efficiency, improved customer satisfaction, and sustainable growth – make this journey worthwhile.

In the end, digital transformation is not just about survival. It's about thriving in a digital age. It's about harnessing the power of technology to create value, drive innovation, and shape the future of business. It's about understanding that in the digital era, change is not only inevitable but also a gateway to limitless possibilities.

Whether you're a startup entrepreneur, a seasoned business executive, or a curious observer, the stories of digital transformation offer valuable lessons. They serve as a reminder that in the world of business, the only constant is change. And in the digital age, those who embrace change are the ones who will lead the way.

DATA-DRIVEN DECISIONS

In the pulsating heart of the business world, decisions are made every day. Some are small, like choosing the brand of coffee for the office; others are monumental, capable of changing the course of a company's future. The question is: how are these decisions made? Are they driven by gut feelings, personal preferences, or perhaps the alignment of stars? The answer, at least for successful businesses, is data.

Data-driven decisions have emerged as the secret weapon of savvy business leaders. They are the compass in the chaotic sea of business, guiding companies towards their goals. Let's delve into the world of data-driven decision-making through a couple of case studies.

Our first case study revolves around a major retail chain that was struggling with inventory management. Their shelves were often stocked with items that didn't sell, while popular products were frequently out of stock. The company decided to turn to data for a solution. They started by collecting data on their sales, customer preferences, and market trends. They then used this data to make decisions about what products to stock and in what quantities. The result was a significant reduction in unsold inventory and a boost in customer satisfaction and sales. The data had spoken, and its advice was invaluable.

In another case, a tech startup was grappling with high employee turnover. The management was puzzled as they offered competitive salaries and benefits. Again, data came to the rescue. The company conducted an internal survey to gather data on employee satisfaction and found that the lack of career development opportunities was the main reason behind the high turnover. Based on this data, the company revamped its policies to provide more growth opportunities for its employees, which resulted in increased employee retention.

These case studies demonstrate the power of data-driven decisions. They can identify problems that may not be apparent on the surface and provide insights into their solutions. However, businesses must remember that data is only as good as the tools and minds interpreting it. It's crucial to have the right analytical tools and a team skilled in data analysis.

Another important aspect is the quality of data. If the data is flawed, the decisions based on it will likely be flawed as well. Therefore, businesses must ensure that their data is accurate, relevant, and up-to-date.

Moreover, while data can guide decisions, it shouldn't replace human judgement. Data can tell you what is happening, but it can't always explain why it's happening. It can provide insights, but it can't understand the nuances of human emotions and behaviours. Therefore, the best decisions are often a combination of data and human intuition.

In conclusion, data-driven decisions are not just a buzzword; they are a powerful tool for businesses. They can provide a clear direction, eliminate guesswork, and lead to more informed, effective decisions. However, businesses must learn to use this tool effectively, ensuring they have the right data, the right tools to analyse it, and the right people to interpret it. If used wisely, data can be the guiding light that leads businesses to success.

Chapter 10
CUSTOMER SERVICE EXCELLENCE

UNDERSTANDING CUSTOMER NEEDS

In the bustling world of commerce, a story unfolded that underscored the paramount importance of understanding customer needs. In the heart of a thriving city existed a well-established company named TechD. TechD was a leader in the tech industry and was known for its innovative products and solutions. However, despite its cutting-edge technology and reputation, the company faced a significant challenge - a steady decline in sales.

The protagonist of this narrative, Tushar, was the newly appointed CEO of TechD. A man of vision and determination, he was keenly aware that in order to reverse the situation, he needed to dive deeper and identify the root cause of the problem. His intuition hinted at a possible disconnect between what the company was offering and what the customers truly wanted.

Tushar decided to initiate a comprehensive research project to understand the customers' needs better. He assembled a team of market researchers, product developers, and customer service representatives. Their mission was clear - to listen to the voice of the customers, understand their needs and expectations, and align the company's offerings accordingly.

The team started by conducting a series of customer interviews and surveys. They also analysed customer reviews and feedback about TechD's products. The data collected was eye-opening. The customers appreciated the innovative nature of the products but found them too complex and difficult to use. They wanted solutions that were simple, user-friendly, and met their specific needs.

Tushar realised that TechD had been so focused on innovation and technology that it had lost sight of its customers' needs. The products were technologically advanced but did not cater to the customers' desire for simplicity and practicality.

Armed with these insights, Tushar decided to take a customer-centric approach. He directed the product development team to design products that were not only technologically superior but also easy to use. He also emphasised the need for excellent customer service to ensure that customers felt heard and valued.

In the following months, TechD launched a new line of user-friendly products. They also improved their customer service and ensured that customer feedback was incorporated into their product development process. The results were astounding. Sales increased, and customer satisfaction levels soared. TechD had successfully turned the tide by understanding and catering to their customers' needs.

This case study of TechD serves as a powerful reminder of the importance of understanding customer needs in business. It underscores the fact that a company's success is not solely dependent on its products or services but also on its ability to understand and meet its customers' needs.

In the end, it is the customers who decide the fate of a product or a company. Therefore, businesses must make an earnest effort to understand their customers, anticipate their needs, and strive to exceed their expectations. This is the key to achieving long-term success and sustainability in the competitive world of business.

So, as we delve deeper into the world of business case studies, remember the story of TechD. Let it be a reminder that in the complex tapestry of business strategies, understanding customer needs is not just a thread but a crucial warp that holds everything together.

DELIVERING QUALITY SERVICE

In the bustling world of commerce, the significance of delivering quality service is a tale that's as old as time yet as relevant as ever. This chapter unfolds the narrative of how businesses, regardless of their size or industry, can leverage this timeless principle to achieve success.

Once upon a time, in a world brimming with businesses, there was a company that was struggling to make a mark. Despite having a strong product portfolio, they were unable to compete effectively in the market. The reason? They were missing out on one crucial aspect – the provision of quality service.

Quality service, as the company soon discovered, was more than just a business jargon. It was an essential ingredient in the recipe for business success, a magical potion that could transform their fortunes. It was about understanding customer needs, exceeding their expectations, and creating an experience that was worth remembering.

The company embarked on a journey to enhance its service quality. They realised that it was not a one-time effort but a continuous process. They started by setting clear service standards. Everyone in the company, from the CEO to the janitor, understood what was expected of them in terms of service delivery. They knew that every interaction with a customer, no matter how small, had the power to shape the customer's perception of their brand.

Next, they focused on employee training. The company understood that their employees were the face of their brand. They invested in regular training programmes to equip their employees with the skills necessary to deliver exceptional service. They encouraged their employees to go the extra mile, to not just satisfy the customers but delight them.

The company also realised the importance of customer feedback. They actively sought out feedback from their customers, making it a point to listen to their praises and criticisms alike. They used this feedback as a compass, guiding them in their journey towards service excellence.

In their quest to deliver quality service, the company also embraced technology. They used it as a tool to streamline their processes, making them more efficient and customer-friendly. They leveraged technology to provide personalised service, understanding that each customer was unique and deserved an experience tailored to their needs.

As the company implemented these changes, they began to see a transformation. Their customers were happier, their employees were more engaged, and their bottom line was healthier. They realised that delivering quality service was not just about making their customers happy but also about improving their business performance.

The company's story serves as an enlightening case study, proving that delivering quality service is not an option but a necessity for businesses. It shows that quality service can be the difference between a business that flourishes and one that flounders. It highlights the fact that quality service is not a cost but an investment that yields significant returns.

In the end, delivering quality service is about creating a culture that values customers. It's about understanding that customers are not just numbers on a spreadsheet but people with expectations and emotions. It's about realising that every interaction with a customer is an opportunity to create a positive impression, an opportunity to tell a story that the customer remembers and cherishes.

The tale of delivering quality service is indeed a compelling one. It's a tale that every business should heed, a tale that underscores the power of service in shaping a business's destiny.

HANDLING CUSTOMER COMPLAINTS

The air was thick with tension as the phone rang in the bustling customer service department of the renowned multinational corporation XYZ Inc. The customer service representative, a young woman named Ishika, adjusted her headset and prepared herself for what was about to unfold. It was a routine she had become accustomed to, but every call was as unpredictable as the last.

On the other end of the line was a disgruntled customer named Mr. Amit. He had recently purchased an expensive home appliance from the company, which had malfunctioned within a week of its purchase. The frustration was evident in his voice, and Ishika knew she was in for a challenging conversation.

Ishika was aware that handling customer complaints was a delicate task, requiring a balanced mix of empathy, patience, and problem-solving skills. She took a deep breath and began to navigate the turbulent sea of Mr. Amit's dissatisfaction.

She listened attentively, allowing him to vent his frustrations without interruption. It was not just about resolving the issue at hand; it was about preserving the company's reputation and ensuring customer satisfaction.

As Ishika listened, she made notes, carefully documenting the details of Mr. Amit's complaint. She knew the importance of accurate record-keeping in managing customer complaints. These notes would not only help her address this particular issue but would also provide valuable insights for the company's product development and quality assurance teams.

Once Mr. Amit had finished detailing his grievances, Ishika expressed her genuine understanding and apologised for the inconvenience he had experienced. It was a sincere apology, not just a corporate script. She then assured him that she would do everything in her power to address his concerns and find a satisfactory resolution.

In the world of customer service, it's crucial to be proactive. Ishika didn't just wait for Mr. Amit to suggest a solution. Instead, she proposed a plan of action. She offered to have the malfunctioning appliance picked up and replaced with a new one, promising to expedite the process to minimise any further inconvenience.

Mr. Amit, though still upset, seemed to appreciate the prompt response. Ishika could sense a slight change in his tone. It was a small victory, but a victory nonetheless.

However, Ishika knew that her job didn't end with the phone call. She immediately sent a detailed report to the relevant departments, emphasising the need for urgent action. She also scheduled a follow-up call with Mr. Amit to ensure that the solution proposed was implemented and that he was satisfied with the resolution.

Handling customer complaints is a crucial aspect of any business. It requires a perfect blend of empathy, listening skills, problem-solving abilities, and prompt action. It's not just about resolving the issue but also about turning an unhappy customer into a satisfied one, thereby preserving the company's reputation and fostering customer loyalty.

In the case of XYZ Inc., Ishika's effective handling of Mr. Amit's complaint not only resolved his immediate problem but also provided valuable insights for the company's future product development. It was a clear demonstration of how effectively handling customer complaints can have far-reaching benefits for a business. This was a real-world lesson that went beyond textbooks, a lesson in empathy, problem-solving, and the art of turning a negative into a positive.

BUILDING CUSTOMER LOYALTY

In the heart of the bustling Pune stood a small bakery, 'Baker's Delight', a jewel amidst the concrete landscape. The aroma of freshly baked bread wafted through the air, tickling the noses of passersby. The owner, Mr. B, had been running the bakery for over two decades. His secret recipe wasn't just the perfect blend of flour and yeast; he had another ingredient, a vital one - customer loyalty.

Mr. B knew that his bakery's success didn't solely depend on the quality of his products. His customers were his most significant assets. He understood the importance of building strong relationships with his customers and fostering a sense of loyalty that would ensure the sustainability and growth of his business.

One day, a young business student named Sam, fascinated by the bakery's success amidst the corporate jungle, approached Mr. B. Sam and asked, "How do you manage to thrive in such a competitive environment?" Mr. B, with a twinkle in his eye, replied, "The secret lies in building customer loyalty."

To explain his strategy, Mr. B shared a story about a loyal customer, Mrs. Devi. She had been buying her daily loaf of bread from 'Baker's Delight' for years. Despite having many other bakeries closer to her home, she chose to travel the extra mile to buy from Mr B's bakery. When Sam asked her why, she replied, "Their bread is indeed delicious, but it's the way they value and treat their customers that keeps me coming back."

Mr. B had always ensured that his customers felt valued. He knew their names, their favourite bread, and even details about their lives. He made it a point to engage with them personally, creating a bond that went beyond a mere business transaction. His customers were not just numbers on a sales report; they were a part of his extended family.

The bakery also had a loyalty programme. For every ten purchases, customers would get a loaf of bread free. This not only incentivised repeat purchases but also made customers feel appreciated for their patronage. Mr. B also ensured that he acted on customer feedback. When a customer suggested that the bakery should start offering whole wheat bread, Mr. B introduced it to the bakery's menu. This move not only expanded his product line but also sent a clear message to his customers - their opinions mattered.

However, building customer loyalty wasn't just about personal interactions and reward programmes. Mr. B was also consistent in delivering quality products. He knew that no amount of personal connection or rewards could compensate for a subpar product. His bakery always used the best ingredients, and his team was trained to uphold the highest standards of service.

As Sam left the bakery, he had learned a valuable lesson. Building customer loyalty was not a one-time effort; it was a continuous process. It required personal connection, acknowledging customer feedback, rewarding loyalty, and, above all, consistently delivering quality. These were the ingredients to Mr B's successful recipe, the secret behind 'Baker's Delight.'

In the world of business, customer loyalty stands as a pillar of success. It is a testament to a company's ability to not just attract customers but also to retain them. As the case of 'Baker's Delight' shows, building customer loyalty is an art that requires a blend of personal connection, quality assurance, and customer appreciation. It is this art that sets successful businesses apart, ensuring their growth and sustainability in the face of competition.

Chapter 11

LEADERSHIP AND MANAGEMENT

EFFECTIVE LEADERSHIP

In the bustling heart of Hyderabad, a giant multinational corporation known as TechCorp was teetering on the brink of failure. The company's stocks had plummeted, employees were leaving in droves, and customers were losing faith. The once-thriving tech giant was in desperate need of a turnaround. The board of directors decided a change in leadership was required, and so they appointed the charismatic and experienced Anand as the new CEO. This change marked the beginning of a fascinating case study on effective leadership.

From the onset, Anand realised that the company's survival hinged on his ability to inspire, motivate, and unite the employees. The atmosphere within the company was thick with fear and uncertainty. He honed in on these feelings, addressing them head-on during his first company-wide meeting. He spoke about the challenges the company was facing and the opportunities that lay ahead. His honesty and transparency were a refreshing change, and it sparked a glimmer of hope within the employees.

Anand understood that effective leadership is not just about making strategic decisions and setting goals. It also involves creating a positive work environment where employees feel valued, respected, and motivated. He initiated regular team meetings, provided constructive feedback, and recognised and rewarded good work. He also made a point to connect with employees on a personal level, taking the time to understand their aspirations, fears, and ideas. This approach fostered a sense of belonging and loyalty among the employees.

Under Anand's leadership, TechCorp also underwent a strategic shift. He realised that the company had been too focused on short-term gains, which led to the neglect of innovation and long-term growth. He steered the company towards investing in research and development and exploring new market opportunities. This strategic change required a lot of courage and foresight, but Anand was willing to take the risk.

One of Anand's most admirable qualities was his ability to make tough decisions. When a project was not delivering the expected results, he was not afraid to pull the plug and redirect resources to more promising ventures. This decisiveness saved the company a significant amount of money and time.

Anand also understood that effective leadership extends beyond the boundaries of the company. He worked hard to rebuild relationships with customers, suppliers, and shareholders. He was transparent about the company's situation and his plans to turn things around. This honesty helped to rebuild trust and confidence among these key stakeholders.

The turnaround of TechCorp under Anand's leadership was nothing short of miraculous. Within a couple of years, the company was back on its feet with rising stock prices, a motivated workforce, and a renewed reputation in the market. This remarkable transformation was a testament to the power of effective leadership.

In conclusion, the case of TechCorp under Anand's leadership provides valuable insights into the critical role of leadership in a business's success. It demonstrates that effective leadership is not just about strategic planning and decision-making. It is also about inspiring and motivating employees, fostering a positive work environment, making tough decisions, and building strong relationships with key stakeholders. This case study serves as a powerful reminder that effective leadership can indeed turn a sinking ship around.

DECISION-MAKING

As the clock ticked in the corner of the room, the board members sat pensively, each immersed in their own thoughts. It was a critical juncture for the company, and the decision they were about to make would steer its course for the foreseeable future. This was a scene that had been repeated countless times in the world of business.

In the realm of business, decision-making is not just a process; it is an art, a science, and sometimes, a high-stakes gamble. It is the fulcrum on which the balance of success and failure rests. Every business case study is a testament to the power of decision-making, and as we delve deeper into this subchapter, we'll explore this concept in its full complexity.

Imagine a chessboard, if you will. Each move made by a player is a decision, a choice made from an array of possibilities. The player must consider the immediate effects of the move, the potential counter-moves by the opponent, and the long-term strategy to checkmate the king. Business is a similar game, albeit with higher stakes and real-world consequences.

Let us take the case of a well-known technology company that was on the brink of bankruptcy in the late '90s. The board made the bold decision to bring back its ousted founder. This decision, fraught with risk, proved to be a masterstroke, leading to a series of innovations that not only saved the company but made it one of the most valuable entities in the world. This is the power of decision-making.

However, decision-making in business is not always about grand gestures or drastic measures. Often, it is about the small, day-to-day choices that shape the culture, operations, and, ultimately, the success of a company. A retail giant's decision to invest in employee training and benefits, for instance, led to improved customer service, increased sales, and a reputation for being an excellent employer.

Decision-making is also about acknowledging and learning from failures. The story of a prominent soft drink manufacturer's failed attempt to change its century-old formula serves as a reminder that understanding customer preferences and sentiments is crucial. The company's quick decision to revert to the original formula, coupled with a humble acknowledgement of the mistake, helped salvage its reputation and market share.

In the labyrinth of business, decision-making is the compass that guides companies. It requires a blend of intuition, experience, foresight, and courage. It demands an understanding of the market, the competition, and the internal dynamics of the company. It involves a fine balance between risk and reward, change and stability, innovation and tradition.

As we journey through this subchapter, we'll explore diverse case studies that highlight the role of decision-making in shaping businesses. We'll delve into the thought processes, the deliberations, the risks, and the outcomes. We'll look at successes and failures, at celebrated decisions and infamous blunders.

Whether it's a startup deciding on its first product, a multinational corporation planning a merger, or a struggling company contemplating a turnaround strategy, decision-making is at the heart of it all. It's a fascinating, complex process that can make or break a company, and it's a journey that we'll embark on together in this subchapter.

Decision-making in business is a saga of choices and consequences, a narrative of risks and rewards. It's a story that's written every day in boardrooms across the world, and it's the story we'll explore in this subchapter. So, let's turn the page and delve into the world of decision-making.

TEAM MANAGEMENT

In the bustling corridors of the corporate world, a skill that often goes unnoticed yet is critically integral to a company's success is the art of team management. It's an orchestra where the conductor, the team manager, must strike a perfect harmony among the diverse instruments and the team members to create a symphony of growth and success.

Once upon a time, XYZ Ltd. was struggling to stay afloat in the competitive market. The CEO, Mr. Shankar, was a dynamic man with a clear vision. However, the discord among his team members was creating a barrier to his vision. The teams were working in silos; each member focused on individual tasks rather than the bigger picture. The inefficiency was palpable, and the company's bottom line was suffering.

Mr. Shankar decided to bring in a professional team manager, Ms. Sanskrit, with a reputation for turning things around. As she stepped into the chaotic office, she knew her task was cut out. The first thing she did was to arrange a team meeting. In the meeting, she encouraged the team members to share their thoughts, concerns, and ideas. It was a cathartic session where everyone felt heard and acknowledged.

Ms. Sanskrit then introduced the concept of team-building activities. She organised a weekend retreat where the team members participated in various fun and challenging tasks. They learned to communicate effectively, trust each other, and work towards a common goal. The weekend was filled with laughter, learning, and a newfound respect for each other.

Back in the office, the changes were evident. There was a sense of camaraderie among the team members. The communication improved, the productivity soared, and the team started working like a well-oiled machine. Ms. Sanskrit didn't stop there. She introduced a system of regular feedback and recognition. The team members felt valued and motivated to work harder.

The transformation was remarkable. The company's performance improved significantly, and Mr. Shankar couldn't be happier. He realised that effective team management was not just about delegating tasks and meeting deadlines. It was about building a cohesive team where everyone felt valued, heard, and motivated to give their best.

The story of XYZ Ltd. is a testament to the power of effective team management. It's about recognising the individual strengths of the team members and leveraging them for the team's success. It's about fostering an environment of trust, collaboration, and mutual respect. It's about aligning the team members with the company's vision and motivating them to work towards it.

In the business world, where competition is intense and the stakes are high, effective team management can be a game-changer. It can turn a struggling company into a thriving one, a group of individuals into a cohesive team, and an ambitious vision into a successful reality.

So, the next time you find yourself in the cacophony of the corporate world, remember the story of XYZ Ltd. Remember that the symphony of success is not just about the individual notes but about the harmony among them. And that, dear readers, is the magic of effective team management.

CHANGE MANAGEMENT

In the world of business, the only constant is change. A successful business not only adapts to change but also takes advantage of it. This chapter of our journey through business case studies introduces us to the intriguing world of change management.

Imagine a multinational corporation, let's call it 'Enterprise X.' This company has a well-established business model, a loyal customer base, and an experienced workforce. But as the winds of change blow, new technologies emerge, disruptive startups challenge the status quo, and customer preferences evolve. Suddenly, Enterprise X finds itself at a crossroads. To survive and thrive, it must adapt, innovate, and transform. This is where the art and science of change management come into play.

Change management is the discipline that guides how we prepare, equip, and support individuals to successfully adopt change to drive organisational success and outcomes. It's about people and how they navigate the choppy waters of transformation. In our case study, we delve into how Enterprise X managed to embrace change and turn challenges into opportunities.

Enterprise X's journey began with recognising the need for change. It was clear that sticking to the old ways of doing things would lead to stagnation and decline. However, acknowledging the need for change and implementing it are two different things. The first major challenge was resistance from within. Employees, comfortable in their routines, were apprehensive about the changes. They feared the unknown, the loss of job security, and the need to learn new skills.

Change management, therefore, starts with communication. Enterprise X's leadership communicated the reasons for change, the benefits it would bring, and how it would be implemented. They sought to reassure employees, involve them in the change process, and provide the necessary training and support. This open, honest, and empathetic communication helped to reduce resistance and foster a positive attitude towards change.

The next step was planning and implementing the changes. This involved setting clear goals, defining roles and responsibilities, and developing a detailed plan of action. The changes were implemented gradually, allowing employees to adapt at their own pace. Regular feedback sessions were held to address concerns and make necessary adjustments.

Throughout this process, Enterprise X faced numerous challenges. There were setbacks, mistakes, and unexpected complications. But with each challenge, the company learned and adapted. It was a process of trial and error, learning from failures, and celebrating successes.

The change management process at Enterprise X was not just about adopting new technologies or changing business processes. It was about creating a culture of continuous learning and improvement. It was about empowering employees to take ownership of the change and become active participants in the transformation process.

In conclusion, the case study of Enterprise X provides valuable insights into the complex and challenging process of change management. It shows how a well-planned and well-executed change management strategy can help businesses adapt to changing environments, improve performance, and achieve long-term success.

Change is inevitable in business. However, effective change management can be a catalyst for growth, innovation, and success. As we continue our journey through business case studies, we will explore other facets of business management, each with its unique challenges and opportunities.

Chapter 12

BUSINESS ETHICS AND SOCIAL RESPONSIBILITY

ETHICAL BUSINESS PRACTICES

In an era where competition is fierce, and profits are paramount, the story of a business that upholds ethical practices holds a unique charm. It's a tale that begins not with a single product or service but with a core set of values. This narrative is about a company that chooses to do the right thing, even when no one is watching.

Once upon a time, in the heart of a bustling city, there existed a small but thriving business named "Honest Enterprises". This company, though not the largest or most lucrative in its industry, was renowned for its unwavering commitment to ethical business practices. This was the cornerstone of its operations, the fundamental principle that guided every decision, big or small.

Honest Enterprises was led by a charismatic and principled leader, Mr. Integrity. Under his stewardship, the company not only achieved financial success but also earned an impeccable reputation. His business was not merely about making money; it was about creating value and making a positive impact on society.

104

Mr. Integrity believed that ethical business practices were not just about following laws and regulations. Rather, it was about fostering a culture of trust, honesty, and respect. He was of the view that ethical practices were not a burden but an opportunity to build a sustainable and successful business.

To ensure the implementation of these values, Mr. Integrity introduced a comprehensive ethical code of conduct within the organisation. He created a transparent system where employees were encouraged to voice their concerns without fear of retribution. The company's dealings with its clients, suppliers, and stakeholders were marked by fairness and honesty. There were no hidden fees, no misleading advertisements, and no exploitation. The company always honoured its commitments and treated everyone with respect and dignity.

However, the road to ethical business practices was not always smooth. There were times when the company faced situations where the easier path would have led to higher profits, but it would have compromised its ethical standards. In such instances, Mr. Integrity never wavered. He firmly believed that short-term gains achieved through unethical means would eventually lead to long-term losses.

One such instance was when Honest Enterprises was offered a lucrative contract, but it came with a condition that they compromise the quality of their products. The deal promised significant financial gains and a chance to outdo their competitors. However, Mr. Integrity declined the offer. He held his ground, choosing to uphold the company's reputation over immediate profits.

This decision was met with criticism from some quarters, but it also earned the company immense respect from its customers and the wider business community. Over time,

Honest Enterprises' commitment to ethical practices helped it build a strong brand identity. It attracted loyal customers who valued the company's integrity and were willing to pay a premium for their products and services.

The story of Honest Enterprises is a compelling testament to the power of ethical business practices. It underlines the fact that businesses can indeed succeed without compromising their principles. It's a narrative that inspires, encourages, and reinforces the belief that ethics and profits are not mutually exclusive but can coexist and complement each other in the realm of business.

In conclusion, the tale of Honest Enterprises serves as a reminder that the path to long-term success in business is paved with ethical practices. It may not be the easiest route, but it is certainly the most rewarding one. For businesses that aspire to make a difference, this narrative serves as a beacon, illuminating the path towards success grounded in ethics and integrity.

CORPORATE SOCIAL RESPONSIBILITY

In the bustling arena of business, there is a rising protagonist that is gradually taking centre stage - Corporate Social Responsibility (CSR). As we delve into this subchapter of our book, "Vyāpār", we will explore this multifaceted character in the world of commerce and its profound impact on the way businesses operate.

Once upon a time, the sole goal of a corporation was to generate profits and provide dividends to its shareholders. However, as the world evolved, so did the expectations from businesses. Society began to demand more from corporations than just financial returns. This heralded the dawn of CSR, a concept that urges companies to consider the interests of all stakeholders – not just shareholders but also employees, customers, communities, and the environment.

The story of CSR is not a fairy tale; it's a saga of transformation. It has gone from being a voluntary initiative to an integral part of a company's strategy. One of the most compelling tales of this transformation is that of the multinational technology company Apple Inc. Once criticised for its environmental practices, Apple has turned the tables by committing to a 100% renewable energy goal. Today, it is recognised as one of the leading tech giants driving sustainability.

Our journey through the world of CSR will also take us to the land of the Swedish furniture giant IKEA. Known for its affordable, assemble-it-yourself furniture, IKEA's CSR narrative is centred on sustainability and creating a better everyday life for people. From investing in renewable energy to sourcing materials from sustainable suppliers, IKEA's story is a testament to the power of CSR in enhancing a company's reputation and customer loyalty.

Yet, CSR does not always entail smooth sailing. There are tales of trials and tribulations, as seen in the case of the British Petroleum (BP) oil spill. The disaster not only caused significant environmental damage but also tarnished BP's image. It served as a grim reminder that neglecting CSR can lead to catastrophic consequences.

The tale of CSR is not confined to large corporations. Small and medium enterprises (SMEs), too, have a role to play. The story of Patagonia, an American outdoor clothing company, proves that even SMEs can make a significant impact. Through its pledge to use sustainable materials and donate a portion of its profits to environmental causes, Patagonia has woven CSR into its brand identity.

As we journey through the CSR landscape, we will also explore the role of regulatory bodies and non-governmental organisations (NGOs). Their growing influence has led to the development of CSR standards and guidelines, pushing companies to be more accountable and transparent.

The narrative of CSR is a saga of change, a testament to the evolution of businesses, and a beacon for the future. It is a story of how businesses can contribute to societal well-being while also fulfilling their economic objectives. As we delve deeper into this subchapter, we will unravel more such fascinating tales of CSR, offering insights into its importance in today's business world.

In the grand scheme of business, CSR is more than just a subchapter in a book; it is a chapter in the story of humanity, a narrative of progress, and a testament to the power of responsible business. It is a story that continues to unfold, and as it does, it is redefining the purpose of business in society.

SUSTAINABILITY IN BUSINESS

As we delve deeper into the complexities of the business world, we are confronted with the concept of sustainability. It is not merely a buzzword that has gained popularity in recent times; it is a critical factor that determines the long-term success of any business. Sustainability in business is essentially about conducting operations in a manner that minimises harm to the environment and promotes social well-being while still generating profits.

We can take the case of Patagonia, an outdoor clothing company, as an example. The company's core mission is to "build the best product, cause no unnecessary harm, and use business to inspire and implement solutions to the environmental crisis." Patagonia has been a pioneer in integrating sustainability into its business operations. From using recycled materials in their products to donating a portion of their profits to environmental causes, Patagonia has proven that a business can be both profitable and sustainable.

However, sustainability is not just about the environment. It also involves social factors and economic stability. For instance, Unilever, a multinational consumer goods company, has set specific targets for improving health, hygiene, and living conditions as part of its sustainable living plan. The company also aims to enhance livelihoods, reduce environmental impact, and source raw materials sustainably. These initiatives have not only improved Unilever's reputation but also boosted its financial performance.

On the other hand, neglecting sustainability can lead to severe consequences. The BP oil spill in 2010 serves as a stark reminder of this. The disaster, resulting from insufficient safety measures, led to an environmental catastrophe that cost the company billions in fines and cleanup costs. Moreover, BP's reputation suffered a massive blow, and its share price plummeted. This incident underscored the importance of adopting sustainable practices in business.

Sustainability in business also involves economic stability. Companies must ensure that their operations are financially sustainable in the long run. This involves careful planning, risk management, and strategic investment. For instance, Apple has a robust financial sustainability strategy that includes a diverse product portfolio, innovative design, and a strong focus on customer satisfaction. This strategy has enabled the company to remain profitable even in challenging economic conditions.

Sustainability is becoming a necessity in the business world. Companies are increasingly realising that sustainable practices can lead to improved brand reputation, customer loyalty, and long-term profitability. However, achieving sustainability is not a one-time effort. It requires continuous commitment and effort from all levels of the organisation.

In conclusion, sustainability in business is a multifaceted concept that involves environmental stewardship, social responsibility, and economic stability. Companies like Patagonia, Unilever, and Apple have shown that integrating sustainability into business operations can lead to significant benefits. However, the journey towards sustainability is not without challenges. It requires a clear vision, strong leadership, and a commitment to continuous improvement. As we move forward, it is clear that sustainability will remain a critical factor in the business world. The companies that can successfully integrate sustainability into their business models will be the ones that thrive in the future.

COMMUNITY ENGAGEMENT

In the bustling landscape of commerce, a thriving business is not an island. It exists within a network, a community, where its actions can ripple outwards and cause significant effects. This is where the concept of community engagement comes into play, becoming an integral part of any successful business strategy.

Once upon a time, in a busy city, there was a small but thriving bakery. The owner, Mrs. Brown, was a warm and friendly woman who believed in the power of her local community. She knew that her bakery's success was not just due to the quality of her cakes and pastries but also due to the support from her neighbourhood.

Mrs Brown understood that community engagement was a two-way street. She made it a point to not only sell her products but also to listen to her customers, understand their needs, and contribute to local events and causes. This wasn't just about fostering goodwill; it was about forming a symbiotic relationship with the community of which her business was a part.

One day, Mrs. Brown noticed that the local school was raising funds for a new playground. She decided to assist by hosting a bake sale wherein all proceeds would go towards the school's cause. The event was a huge success, not just in terms of the funds raised but also in strengthening the bond between her bakery and the community.

The bake sale had a ripple effect. It increased awareness about the bakery, brought in new customers, and deepened the loyalty of existing ones. Moreover, it helped the school achieve its goal of a new playground. This was community engagement at its best, a win-win situation for both the business and the community.

However, community engagement is not just about hosting events or donating to causes. It's about being a responsible entity within the community. This is something Mrs Brown demonstrated when she decided to switch to sustainable packaging for her products. She was aware of the growing concern about plastic waste and wanted her business to be part of the solution, not the problem.

This decision was met with overwhelming support from the community. Not only did it reinforce the bakery's image as a responsible business, but it also triggered a chain of changes within the community. Other businesses followed suit, leading to a significant reduction in plastic waste. Mrs Brown's bakery became a role model for other businesses, showing how community engagement could drive positive change.

In the end, Mrs. Brown's approach towards community engagement not only boosted her bakery's success but also enriched the community. Her story serves as a case study, demonstrating how businesses can thrive by engaging with their communities. It shows that community engagement is not just about giving back but also about fostering relationships, driving positive change, and creating a sustainable ecosystem where businesses and communities can thrive together.

Community engagement, as highlighted by Mrs. Brown's bakery, is not a mere optional strategy for businesses. It is a necessity, a cornerstone for business growth and sustainability. It is a powerful tool that can shape business narratives, influence customer perceptions, and drive positive societal change. As businesses navigate the complex landscape of the 21st century, community engagement will continue to be a critical factor in their journey towards success.

Chapter 13

THE ROAD TO SUCCESS

ACHIEVING BUSINESS GOALS

As the story of our Vy*āp*ā*r* unfolds, we find ourselves in the labyrinth of achieving business goals. The path to these goals is often obscured by the complexities of market dynamics, shifting consumer preferences, and the constant need for innovation. Yet, in our exploration, we discover that the key to navigating this labyrinth lies in a well-defined strategy, a clear vision, and an unwavering commitment to execution.

Imagine a business as a ship embarking on a voyage. The business goals would be its destination. However, setting sail without a course or a map would lead to aimless drifting or, even worse, shipwreck. In the same vein, a business without clear goals or a plan to achieve them is likely to flounder. Therefore, the first step in our journey to achieving business goals is to set them. These goals, much like a distant shoreline, provide a direction and a purpose. They inspire and motivate the team, driving them forward through the stormy seas of business challenges.

Once the goals are set, the next step is to map out the course. This is where strategic planning comes into play. A well-crafted strategy is like a compass, guiding the business through the tumultuous market conditions and competitive forces. It helps identify the most efficient and effective route to the destination, considering the current position, resources, and capabilities of the business. It also includes contingency plans for unexpected obstacles or changes in the business environment, ensuring that the business remains on course even amidst uncertainty.

However, having a strategy is not enough. Much like a ship's crew must work together to steer the ship, so must the entire business organisation collaborate to execute the strategy. Each member of the team plays a crucial role, from the CEO setting the vision to the frontline employees interacting with the customers. Achieving business goals requires a collective effort, with everyone pulling in the same direction. It also requires strong leadership to keep the team motivated, focused, and aligned with the business objectives.

In our exploration of business case studies, we come across numerous examples of businesses that have successfully achieved their goals. From startups that have disrupted industries to established corporations that have adapted to change and sustained their success, these businesses share common characteristics. They have clear, measurable goals that are aligned with their vision and mission. They have robust strategies that are responsive to the market dynamics and their internal capabilities. They have a culture of execution, where everyone understands their role and contributes to the achievement of the business goals.

However, achieving business goals is not a one-time event. It is an ongoing process that requires continuous monitoring, evaluation, and adjustment. The business landscape is constantly evolving, and businesses must adapt their goals and strategies accordingly. They must also learn from their successes and failures, using these insights to refine their approach and improve their performance.

In conclusion, achieving business goals is a journey, not a destination. It is a journey that requires setting a clear direction, crafting a robust strategy, fostering a culture of execution, and continuously learning and adapting. It is a journey that, despite its challenges, can lead to significant growth, success, and fulfilment. So, as we delve deeper into our business case studies, let us keep these insights in mind and explore how businesses navigate their way to their goals.

LEARNING FROM MISTAKES

In the corporate landscape, where a multitude of factors determine the rise or fall of an enterprise, one of the most impactful lessons is often learned from mistakes. They are not the end of the road but rather stepping stones that can propel a business towards success if navigated wisely.

One such example is that of Ford, the automobile giant, whose launch of the Edsel model in 1958 was a failure of epic proportions. It was a product of extensive market research and a budget of $400 million, yet it was met with a calamitous reception. The Edsel was a costly mistake that resulted in losses amounting to $350 million. This setback, however, became a turning point for Ford. It served as a harsh reminder that consumer demand and preferences cannot be predicted with absolute certainty and that it is critical to remain flexible and adaptable. Ford learned to listen more attentively to the market, leading to the successful launch of the Mustang in 1964, a car that has since become an iconic symbol of the brand.

Another intriguing case is that of Kodak, the once-dominant leader in the photography industry. Despite inventing the digital camera in 1975, Kodak made the grave error of underestimating its potential impact. This misjudgment led to the company's steady decline and eventual bankruptcy in 2012. However, Kodak managed to learn from its mistakes and adapt. It shifted focus towards new areas like printing, imaging for business, and film for the movie industry. Today, Kodak's story serves as a stark reminder of the importance of embracing innovation and adapting to technological changes.

In the realm of technology, Microsoft's initial failure in the smartphone market is a classic example. Despite being a pioneer with its Windows Mobile platform, Microsoft failed to anticipate the shift towards app-based ecosystems, leading to the dominance of Google's Android and Apple's iOS. However, the company learned a valuable lesson about the importance of staying ahead of market trends and user preferences. This understanding led Microsoft to pivot towards cloud computing and artificial intelligence, areas where it now holds a substantial market share.

There's also the story of Airbnb, which initially struggled to gain traction. The company's original concept was to offer air mattresses and breakfast in the host's living room, but it failed to attract significant interest. The founders learned from this failure and pivoted to a model that allowed hosts to rent out their entire home or apartment. This shift, based on their early missteps, catapulted Airbnb to become a disruptive force in the hospitality industry.

Each of these business case studies paints a vivid picture of how mistakes, while initially detrimental, can serve as powerful catalysts for growth and innovation. They underscore the importance of adaptability, resilience, and the willingness to learn from failures. The road to success is seldom a straight line; it is a winding path filled with trials, errors, and, most importantly, lessons learned. In the end, it isn't about avoiding mistakes but rather about turning them into stepping stones towards success. After all, in the business world, the most profound lessons are often learned not from success but from failure.

CELEBRATING SUCCESS

The sun was setting, casting long shadows over the bustling office. Employees, still glued to their screens, were wrapping up their day, their fingers dancing on the keyboards. The air was thick with anticipation and excitement. The reason? A major project had just been completed successfully, and the company was preparing to celebrate this milestone.

In the corner office, the CEO, a man of few words but immense vision, looked out at his team. He thought about the journey they had undertaken, the obstacles they had overcome, and the success they had achieved. His heart swelled with pride. He knew that this success was not his alone but a collective effort of every individual in the room.

The project had been a challenging one. It required dedication, commitment, and countless hours of work. There were times when the team had hit a wall when they had doubted their ability to deliver. But they persevered, they pushed through the hardships, and they emerged victorious. The CEO knew that this success deserved to be celebrated, not just for the accomplishment itself but for the journey that led to it.

And so, he decided to throw a grand celebration. He wanted it to be a day of joy and appreciation, a day where each member could bask in the glory of their achievement. He wanted to create an atmosphere of camaraderie and shared triumph, where every person felt valued and recognised for their contributions.

The day of the celebration finally arrived. The office was transformed into a festive venue, with balloons, banners, and streamers adorning every corner. A large banner that read "Congratulations, Team!" hung proudly in the reception area. The CEO, donning a party hat, was the first to arrive. He went around the room, shaking hands, patting backs, and expressing his gratitude to each member.

The celebration was in full swing. There was laughter, cheers, and a sense of accomplishment that filled the air. Stories of the journey were shared, anecdotes of the tough times were laughed at, and the success was relished by all.

The CEO took the stage and gave a heartfelt speech, thanking each team member for their hard work and dedication. He spoke of the journey, the challenges, and the triumph. His words echoed the sentiment of every person in the room.

The team left the celebration with a sense of pride and achievement. They felt valued, appreciated, and motivated to take on new challenges. The celebration had not just marked the successful completion of a project, but it had also reinforced the team spirit, the shared vision, and the collective effort that had led to this success.

In the world of business, success can often be a solitary journey. But in this company, success was a shared experience, a collective achievement. The CEO knew the importance of celebrating success by acknowledging the hard work and dedication of his team. He understood that this celebration was not just about a completed project but about the journey, the team, and the shared triumph. And so, in this corner office, amidst the hustle and bustle, success was celebrated, achievements were recognised, and a team was united in their triumph.

LOOKING AHEAD

In the realm of business, the future is a vast ocean of possibilities, filled with potential opportunities and challenges. As we navigate this sea, it is crucial to keep our eyes on the horizon, looking ahead to anticipate what may come. This is the essence of strategic planning and foresight, two key components of successful business management.

As we delve deeper into the realm of business case studies, it becomes more apparent that the businesses that thrive and succeed are the ones that are not only reactive but also proactive. They do not merely respond to changes in the market; they anticipate them. They do not just react to trends; they set them. These businesses understand that the future is not something to be feared or avoided but something to be embraced and shaped.

Looking ahead, therefore, is not just about predicting the future. It's about creating it. It's about taking the raw materials of present circumstances and moulding them into a future that aligns with the business's goals and objectives. This is the kind of forward-thinking approach that sets apart the successful businesses from the unsuccessful ones.

For instance, consider the case of a technology company that foresaw the rise of smartphones and invested heavily in developing apps and mobile-friendly software. This company was not just reacting to a trend; it was shaping the future of its industry. This forward-looking approach paid off handsomely, as the company was well-positioned to capitalise on the smartphone boom when it happened.

On the other hand, consider the case of a retail company that failed to anticipate the rise of e-commerce and online shopping. This company was caught off guard by the shift in consumer behaviour and struggled to adapt. Its lack of foresight cost it dearly, as it lost market share to more nimble competitors that had seen the trend coming and prepared accordingly.

These case studies underscore the importance of looking ahead in business. They highlight the need for strategic planning and foresight to have a vision of the future and work towards it. They remind us that the future is not something to be passively awaited but actively shaped.

Looking ahead, therefore, is a critical skill for any business leader. It involves analysing trends, forecasting changes, and making strategic decisions based on these insights. It involves thinking creatively and innovatively, imagining new possibilities and pushing the boundaries of what is possible. It involves taking risks and making bold moves, even when the path forward is uncertain.

In conclusion, looking ahead is not just about seeing the future; it's about shaping it. It's about taking the initiative and seizing the opportunities that the future holds. As we continue to explore the world of business case studies, let us remember this important lesson. Let us keep our eyes on the horizon, looking ahead with anticipation and excitement. For in the realm of business, the future is a vast ocean of possibilities, and it is ours to shape.

Epilogue

As we draw the curtains on this enlightening journey through the labyrinth of entrepreneurship, we take a moment to reflect on the invaluable insights that these business case studies have provided. Each chapter was a testament to the indomitable spirit of entrepreneurship, the courage to navigate uncharted territories, and the resilience to turn failures into stepping stones for success.

From the initial spark of an idea to the triumph of its successful execution, we have delved into the intricacies of the entrepreneurial journey. We have observed how these extraordinary individuals have defied norms, challenged conventions, and dared to dream big. We have seen how they have wrestled with uncertainties, embraced risks, and emerged victorious against all odds.

These case studies have not merely been stories of businesses; they have been narratives of human endeavour, perseverance, and triumph. They have demonstrated that entrepreneurship is not just about making profits; it is about creating value, transforming lives, and making a difference in the world.

We have learned that success is not a destination but a journey filled with lessons, challenges, and opportunities. The entrepreneurial journey is a roller coaster ride, with its highs and lows, twists and turns. However, as these case studies have shown, it is the journey that shapes the entrepreneur, and it is the journey that truly matters.

As we conclude this book, we hope that these case studies have inspired you, enlightened you, and empowered you to embark on your entrepreneurial journey. Remember, every great business was once a simple idea. It was the courage, determination, and resilience of the entrepreneur that turned that idea into a success story.

May the lessons from these case studies guide you on your journey, empower you to overcome your challenges, and inspire you to turn your idea into a success story. Thank you for joining us on this journey through the world of entrepreneurship. The road to success is always under construction, and we hope this book has provided you with the necessary tools to build your path.

REFERENCES

1. "Netflix vs Blockbuster." Business Wars. Spotify. Accessed March 19, 2024. URL: https:// open.spotify.com/ episode/1it9SpNQQ4VmbwWipKj52o?si=ZHv_61h JSriBhUVsYvE86A&context=spotify%3Ashow %3A6 RbJ UsaOaboq SBqQUfdQtR.

2. "Nike vs Adidas." Business Wars, Spotify, Accessed March19,2024.https://open.spotify.com/episode/ 2gTD uPKW9Ad9I dODuKwxwk?si= PCZPar8dTaCt-zbWC6Xeug.

3. "Inside Amazon's Growth Strategy." HBR on Strategy, Spotify, Accessed March 19, 2024. https://open.spotify. com/episode/4Vg1wkodD8lNTlJHj4ErZu?si=n2r3jvl DRF W7XPg8j5xPSw.

4. Lashinsky, Adam. Inside Apple: How America's Most Admired--and Secretive--Company Really Works. New York: Business Plus, 2012.

5. Isaacson, Walter. Steve Jobs. New York: Simon & Schuster, 2011.

6. Stanford Graduate School of Business. "Zappos.com: Developing a Supply Chain to Deliver WOW!." Stanford Graduate School of Business Case. Stanford University, 2007.

7.　Casadesus-Masanell, Ramon, and Forest L. Reinhardt. "Patagonia." Harvard Business School Case 712-490, June 2012.

8.　"A Case Study of Apple's Supply Chain." Australian Institute of Company Directors (AICD). Accessed March 19, 2024. https://www.aicd.com.au/risk-management/framework/plan/a-case-study-of-apples-supply-chain.html.

9.　Bartleby: Accessed March 19, 2024. https://www.bartleby.com/essay/Apple-Case-Study-Globalization-and-Technology-Change-FKVGD6PMZRFS.

10.　"Impact of Globalization on Apple Inc." Scribd, Accessed March 19, 2024. https://www.scribd.com/doc/61951649/Impact-of-Globalization-on-Apple-Inc.

11.　Frier, Sarah. "The Inside Story of How Facebook Acquired Instagram." Medium, August 5, 2020. Accessed March 19, 2024. https://onezero.medium.com/the-inside-story-of-how-facebook-acquired-instagram-318f244f1283.

12.　Taneja, Yash. "Kodak Bankruptcy: A Case Study." StartupTalky, November 6, 2021. Accessed March 19, 2024. https://startuptalky.com/kodak-bankruptcy-case-study/.

13.　Goswami, Chayanika, and Manisha Mishra. "Spotify Success Story." StartupTalky, October 13, 2023. Accessed March 19, 2024. https://startuptalky.com/spotify_success_story/.

14.　Chau, Justin. "How Starbucks Failed in Australia." Justologist. September 12, 2023. Accessed March 19, 2024. https://www.justologist.com/how-starbucks-failed-in-australia/amp/.

15. Dubey, Riya. "The Successful Corporate Marriage: Merger of Walt Disney and Pixar." IPleaders Blog, July 8, 2021. Accessed March 19, 2024. https://blog.ipleaders.in/the-successful-corporate-marriage-merger-of-walt-disney-and-pixar/

16. Arango, Tim. "How the AOL-Time Warner Merger Went So Wrong." New York Times, January 10, 2010. Accessed March 19, 2024. https://www.nytimes.com/2010/01/11/business/media/11merger.html

17. Keyes, Daniel. "Amazon And Whole Foods Have Not Upended Grocery." Business Insider, June 17, 2019. Accessed March 19, 2024. https://www.businessinsider.com/amazon-whole-foods-have-not-upended-grocery-2019-6?amp

18. Urrutia, Kevin. "Coca-Cola Marketing Strategy." VOY Media. Published February 9, 2024. Accessed March 19, 2024. https://voymedia.com/coca-cola-marketing-strategy/#google_vignette

19. Ravulakollu, Narender. "Data-driven growth: Lessons from Domino's Pizza." AlmaBetter Bytes, July 27, 2023. Accessed March 19, 2024. https://www.almabetter.com/bytes/articles/data-driven-growth-lessons-from-dominos-pizza.

20. Webb, Tim. "BP Response to Oil Spill Fails to Halt Slide in Shares." The Guardian, June 1, 2010. Accessed March 21, 2024. https://amp.theguardian.com/business/2010/jun/01/bp-response-oil-spill-tony-hayward.